Company's Coming®

Greatest Hits

Dips, Spreads & Dressings

visit our **web-site!**
www.companyscoming.com

Over 200 selected recipes by

Jean Paré

Dips, Spreads & Dressings

First printing April 1999

Canadian Cataloguing in Publication Data
Paré, Jean
Greatest Hits: dips, spreads & dressings

Issued also in French under title: Jean Paré grands
succès : trempettes, tartinades et sauces à salade.
Includes index.
ISBN 1-896891-03-9

1. Dips (Appetizers) 2. Cookery (Salad dressing)
3. Appetizers. I. Title. II. Title: Dips, spreads &
dressings. III. Title: Dips, spreads and dressings.

TX740.P347 1999   641.8'12   C98-9011135-6

Published simultaneously in Canada and the United
States of America by
The Recipe Factory Inc. in conjunction with
Company's Coming Publishing Limited
2311 - 96 Street, Edmonton, Alberta,
Canada T6N 1G3
Tel: 780 • 450-6223
Fax: 780 • 450-1857
www.companyscoming.com

Company's Coming is a registered trademark owned
by Company's Coming Publishing Limited

Dips, Spreads & Dressings was created thanks to the
dedicated efforts of the people and organizations listed
below.

COMPANY'S COMING PUBLISHING LIMITED

Author	Jean Paré
President	Grant Lovig
V.P., Product Development	Kathy Knowles
Publishing Coordinator	Marlene Crosbie
Production Coordinator	Jaclyn Draker
Copywriting	Debbie Dixon
Design	Nora Cserny
	Jaclyn Draker

THE RECIPE FACTORY INC.

Research & Development Manager	Nora Prokop
Test Kitchen Supervisor	Lynda Elsenheimer
Editor	Stephanie Amodio
Assistant Editor/Food Stylist	Suzanne Hartman
Proofreader	Mimi Tindall
Photographer	Stephe Tate Photo
Prop Stylist	Gabriele McEleney

Color separations, printing, and binding by
Friesens, Altona, Manitoba, Canada
Printed in Canada

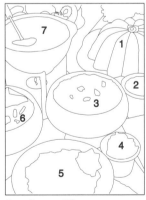

FRONT COVER:

1. Salmon Mousse, page 82
2. Orange Bagel Spread, page 90
3. Guacamole, page 9
4. Parsley Butter, page 57
5. Sour Cream Dip, page 38
6. Simple Picante Salsa, page 10
7. Chocolate Fondue Sauce, page 22

Props Courtesy Of:
La Cache, Le Gnome,
The Glasshouse

visit our web-site!
www.companyscoming.com

table of contents

our cookbooks

COMPANY'S COMING SERIES

150 Delicious Squares
Casseroles
Muffins & More
Salads
Appetizers
Desserts
Soups & Sandwiches
Holiday Entertaining
Cookies
Vegetables
Main Courses
Pasta
Cakes
Barbecues
Dinners of the World
Lunches
Pies
Light Recipes
Microwave Cooking
Preserves
Light Casseroles
Chicken, Etc.
Kids Cooking
Fish & Seafood
Breads
Meatless Cooking
Cooking for Two
Breakfasts & Brunches
Slow Cooker Recipes
Pizza!
One-Dish Meals - NEW
   (August 1999)

SELECT SERIES

Sauces & Marinades
Ground Beef
Beans & Rice
30-Minute Meals
Make-Ahead Salads
No-Bake Desserts

LOW-FAT SERIES

Low-fat Cooking
Low-fat Pasta

GREATEST HITS

Biscuits, Muffins & Loaves
Dips, Spreads & Dressings

INDIVIDUAL TITLES

Company's Coming for Christmas
Easy Entertaining
Beef Today!
Kids - Snacks
Kids - Lunches

the jean paré story

ean Paré grew up understanding that the combination of family, friends and home cooking is the essence of a good life. From her mother she learned to appreciate good cooking, while her father praised even her earliest attempts. When she left home she took with her many acquired family recipes, her love of cooking and her intriguing desire to read recipe books like novels!

In 1963, when her four children had all reached school age, Jean volunteered to cater to the 50th anniversary of the Vermilion School of Agriculture, now Lakeland College. Working out of her home, Jean prepared a dinner for over 1,000 people which launched a flourishing catering operation that continued for over eighteen years. During that time she was provided with countless opportunities to test new ideas with immediate feedback—resulting in empty plates and contented customers! Whether preparing cocktail sandwiches for a house party or serving a hot meal for 1,500 people, Jean Paré earned a reputation for good food, courteous service and reasonable prices.

"Why don't you write a cookbook?" Time and again, as requests for her recipes mounted, Jean was asked that question. Jean's response was to team up with her son, Grant Lovig, in the fall of 1980 to form Company's Coming Publishing Limited. April 14, 1981, marked the debut of 150 DELICIOUS SQUARES, the first Company's Coming cookbook in what soon would become Canada's most popular cookbook series.

Jean Paré's operation has grown steadily from the early days of working out of a spare bedroom in her home. Full-time staff includes marketing personnel located in major cities across Canada. Home Office is based in Edmonton, Alberta in a modern building constructed specially for the company.

Today the company distributes throughout Canada and the United States in addition to numerous overseas markets, all under the guidance of Jean's daughter, Gail Lovig. Best-sellers many times over, Company's Coming cookbooks are published in English and French, plus a Spanish-language edition is available in Mexico. Familiar and trusted in home kitchens the world over, Company's Coming cookbooks are offered in a variety of formats, including the original softcover series.

Jean Paré's approach to cooking has always called for quick and easy recipes using everyday ingredients. Even when travelling, she is constantly on the lookout for new ideas to share with her readers. At home, she can usually be found researching and writing recipes, or working in the company's test kitchen. Jean continues to gain new supporters by adhering to what she calls "the golden rule of cooking": never share a recipe you wouldn't use yourself. It's an approach that works—*millions of times over!*

foreword

ith *Dips, Spreads & Dressings* on your cookbook shelf, you have at your fingertips a wonderfully diverse collection of instant recipe ideas to serve family and friends.

Dips are such a practical appetizer because they can usually be prepared the night before or the morning of your planned event. Offer guests a plate of seasonal ripe fruit accompanied by a sweet cream cheese dip or an elegant presentation of cold shrimp and scallops served with a spicy curry dunk. Who can resist a savory dip surrounded by a colorful array of crunchy cut-up vegetables or that simple age-old favorite, a bowl of chips!

Among the recipes for spreads, you'll find decorative appetizers, crowd-pleasing sandwiches and flavorful jams and jellies to enhance any breakfast or buffet table. Our sandwich and appetizer spreads offer everything from familiar egg salad to exotic smoked salmon or lobster spreads. A melt-in-the-mouth mousse or buttery pâté can be made ahead of time, ready to unmold and serve with a basketful of crackers as guests walk in the door.

Included in our *Jams, Jellies and Marmalades* sections are a variety of old-fashioned favorites and inventive new ideas. Tease your guests' appetites with an addictive appetizer of *Jalapeño Jelly* spooned over cream cheese. Wake up your morning senses with some glamorous *Gooseberry Jam* or *Ginger Pear Marmalade* topping the breakfast bran muffins. Family and friends will appreciate a decorated gift jar of any of our zesty spreads.

What can be said about a spectacular dressing, except that a salad just isn't complete without one. In this section, you'll find a selection of creamy and oil-based recipes to complement any kind of salad you have planned. Included are variations on some of the more traditional recipes which are so simple to prepare you'll soon be crossing store-bought salad dressings off your grocery list!

No matter what the occasion, *Dips, Spreads & Dressings* offers a classic collection of inspiring recipes that you will treasure, and family, friends and guests are certain to love.

each recipe

has been analyzed using the most updated version of the Canadian Nutrient File from Health and Welfare Canada, which is based upon the United States Department of Agriculture (USDA) Nutrient Data Base.

Margaret Ng, B.Sc. (Hon), M.A.
Registered Dietician

Chip Dips

*N*othing says entertaining more than chips and dip. Choose something simple for casual get-togethers such as *Dill Dip* and *Black Bean Dip*, and for more elegant occasions, *King Artichoke Dip* or *Hot Broccoli Dip*. All are very easy to whip up at a moment's notice for everyone to enjoy.

KING ARTICHOKE DIP

Yummy! Wonderful blend of bacon, artichoke, cheese and spinach. Looks pretty too. Great with tortilla chips but also works well with chunks of French bread.

Bacon slices (about ½ lb., 225 g), diced	8	8
Finely chopped onion	1 cup	250 mL
Garlic cloves, minced	2	2
Canned artichoke hearts, drained and chopped	14 oz.	398 mL
Cream cheese, softened	8 oz.	250 g
Sour cream	½ cup	125 mL
Bunch fresh spinach, finely chopped	1	1
Worcestershire sauce	¼ tsp.	1 mL
Milk (optional)		

Sauté bacon, onion and garlic in large frying pan until bacon is cooked and onion is soft. Add artichoke. Sauté for 1 minute.

Beat cream cheese and sour cream together in medium bowl until smooth. Add bacon mixture. Stir.

Mix in spinach and Worcestershire sauce. Thin with milk if desired. Makes 3 cups (750 mL).

2 tbsp. (30 mL): 79 Calories; 6.8 g Total Fat; 137 mg Sodium; 2 g Protein; 2 g Carbohydrate; 1 g Dietary Fiber

SHRIMP AND ARTICHOKE DIP

A chunky dip or spread. Mild but flavorful.

Cream cheese, softened	4 oz.	125 g
Salad dressing (or mayonnaise)	½ cup	125 mL
Sour cream	½ cup	125 mL
Chopped green onion	¼ cup	60 mL
Salt	½ tsp.	2 mL
Pepper	⅛ tsp.	0.5 mL
Canned artichoke hearts, drained and finely chopped	14 oz.	398 mL
Canned broken shrimp, drained	4 oz.	113 g

Beat cream cheese, salad dressing, sour cream, green onion, salt and pepper together in medium bowl.

Add artichoke and shrimp. Stir together. Makes 2¾ cups (675 mL).

2 tbsp. (30 mL): 64 Calories; 5.4 g Total Fat; 150 mg Sodium; 2 g Protein; 2 g Carbohydrate; 1 g Dietary Fiber

CHILI CON QUESO

Chilee-cahn-KAY-soh is a mild cream cheese dip served warm with tortilla chips. Just as delicious with potato chips. Excellent.

Process cheese loaf (such as Velveeta), cut into chunks	1 lb.	500 g
Light cream (half-and-half)	¾ cup	175 mL
Canned chopped green chilies, drained	4 oz.	114 mL
Finely chopped green pepper	¼ cup	60 mL
Chopped pimiento	4 tsp.	20 mL

Place cheese in top of double boiler. Add cream and green chilies. Microwave green pepper on high (100%) for 2 minutes, or boil until tender-crisp. Add to cheese mixture along with pimiento. Melt together, stirring frequently. Heat slowly. If heated too fast or too hot, cheese may become stringy. Serve warm with tortilla chips. Your own are best. Better to make a day ahead so flavors blend. Makes about 3 cups (750 mL).

2 tbsp. (30 mL): 76 Calories; 5.7 g Total Fat; 376 mg Sodium; 4 g Protein; 2 g Carbohydrate; trace Dietary Fiber

Pictured on page 17.

When choosing avocados, select those with full necks and a body that gives a bit when gently squeezed. Store in the refrigerator for up to one week. Cut portions should be sprinkled with lemon or lime juice to prevent browning if you are not using them immediately.

GUACAMOLE

A good dip for tortilla chips or chicken wings.

Avocados, peeled and mashed	2	2
Ripe medium tomato, seeded and finely diced	1	1
Lemon juice	2 tbsp.	30 mL
Minced onion	2 tbsp.	30 mL
Salt	½ tsp.	2 mL

Combine all 5 ingredients in small bowl. Stir together. Makes about 1 cup (250 mL).

2 tbsp. (30 mL): 83 Calories; 7.5 g Total Fat; 169 mg Sodium; 1 g Protein; 5 g Carbohydrate; 2 g Dietary Fiber

Pictured on front cover.

Variation: Stir in ½ tsp. (2 mL) chili powder. Guacamole will darken slightly but it is very good.

GUACAMOLE DIP

A touch of Mexico. Serve with corn chips, tortilla chips or fresh vegetables.

Avocados, peeled and mashed	2	2
Lemon juice	2 tbsp.	30 mL
Onion flakes	2 tsp.	10 mL
Salt	1 tsp.	5 mL
Pepper	¼ tsp.	1 mL
Cayenne pepper	¼ tsp.	1 mL
Garlic powder	¼ tsp.	1 mL
Ripe medium tomato, diced	1	1
Chopped fresh parsley, for garnish (optional)		

Mix all 8 ingredients in small bowl.

Garnish with parsley. Makes about 1 cup (250 mL).

2 tbsp. (30 mL): 84 Calories; 7.5 g Total Fat; 332 mg Sodium; 1 g Protein; 5 g Carbohydrate; 2 g Dietary Fiber

MEXICAN BEAN DIP

No need to travel to get a good dip. Guests will devour this in no time. Serve with assorted tortilla chips and crackers.

Cream cheese, softened	8 oz.	250 g
Sour cream	1 cup	250 mL
Canned refried beans	14 oz.	398 mL
Onion flakes	1 tbsp.	15 mL
Chopped chives	1 tbsp.	15 mL
Parsley flakes	1 tbsp.	15 mL
Chili powder	2 tbsp.	30 mL
Grated medium or sharp Cheddar cheese	1½ cups	375 mL
Grated Monterey Jack cheese	1½ cups	375 mL
Chili powder, generous measure	2 tbsp.	30 mL
Green pimiento-stuffed olives, for garnish		

Mix first 7 ingredients well in medium bowl. Spread in ungreased 3 quart (3 L) shallow casserole dish.

Sprinkle with Cheddar cheese and then Monterey Jack cheese. Sprinkle second amount of chili powder over top. May be chilled at this point until needed. Bake, uncovered, in 350°F (175°C) oven for about 20 minutes until hot.

Garnish with green olives. Makes about 6 cups (1.5 L).

2 tbsp. (30 mL): 64 Calories; 4.9 g Total Fat; 101 mg Sodium; 3 g Protein; 2 g Carbohydrate; 1 g Dietary Fiber

Pictured on page 17.

PICANTE SALSA

The heat in this chunky salsa is adjustable. Simply add more or less jalapeño peppers. Serve with nachos that have melted cheese, sour cream and green onion on them. Also good with quesadillas and sour cream or burgers.

Ripe tomatoes, scalded and peeled, stem ends and cores removed, chopped	4¹/₂ lbs.	2 kg
Canned whole green chilies, drained and chopped	3	3
Large Spanish onion, chopped	1	1
Large green pepper, chopped	1	1
Medium red pepper, chopped	1	1
Canned whole jalapeño peppers, drained and chopped	3-6	3-6
Tomato paste	5¹/₂ oz.	156 mL
White vinegar	³/₄ cup	175 mL
Brown sugar, packed	¹/₄ cup	60 mL
Coarse (pickling) salt	1 tbsp.	15 mL
Paprika	2 tsp.	10 mL
Garlic powder (or 2 cloves, minced)	¹/₂ tsp.	2 mL

Combine all 12 ingredients in large saucepan. Bring to a boil, stirring occasionally. Boil gently for 1 hour, stirring occasionally, until thickened to desired consistency. Close to end of cooking, taste to see if you would like to add more jalapeño pepper. Add as many more as you like. Fill hot sterilized pint jars to within ¹/₂ inch (12 mm) of top. Place sterilized metal lids on jars and screw metal bands on securely. For added assurance against spoilage, you may choose to process in a boiling water bath for 5 minutes. Makes 5 pints (10 cups, 2.5 L).

2 tbsp. (30 mL): 11 Calories; 0.1 g Total Fat; 121 mg Sodium; trace Protein; 3 g Carbohydrate; trace Dietary Fiber

SIMPLE PICANTE SALSA

For a mild, chunky salsa, simply omit the dried crushed chilies. For hot salsa, add more. Easy to double.

Canned tomatoes, with juice, chopped (see Note)	28 oz.	796 mL
Tomato sauce	7¹/₂ oz.	213 mL
Garlic clove, minced	1	1
Small green pepper, chopped	1	1
Small red pepper, chopped	1	1
Dried whole oregano	¹/₂ tsp.	2 mL
Coarse (pickling) salt	¹/₂ tsp.	2 mL
Dried crushed chilies	¹/₂ tsp.	2 mL

Combine all 8 ingredients in large saucepan. Bring to a boil. Boil gently for about 20 minutes, stirring occasionally, until thickened. Cool. Pour into freezer containers to within 1 inch (2.5 cm) of top. Cover with tight fitting lid. Freeze. Makes 3 cups (750 mL).

2 tbsp. (30 mL): 11 Calories; 0.1 g Total Fat; 160 mg Sodium; trace Protein; 2 g Carbohydrate; 1 g Dietary Fiber

Pictured on front cover.

Note: 2¹/₃ lbs. (1 kg) fresh tomatoes can be substituted. Scald, peel and remove cores and stem ends. Dice. Cook as above.

Be creative when deciding what to serve with these savory dips. For instance, a wide variety of tortilla chips are available that offer different color, flavor and fat content. As an alternative, serve chunks of French or pita bread, or a basket of assorted crackers.

SALSA CRUDA

SAHL-sah CROO-dah is an authentic Mexican red sauce. This is a milder uncooked sauce. Use as a sauce or serve with corn chips.

Ripe medium tomatoes, diced	2	2
Minced onion	1/2 cup	125 mL
Green onions, chopped	2	2
Cooking oil	1 tbsp.	15 mL
Granulated sugar	1 tsp.	5 mL
Salt	1/2 tsp.	2 mL
Canned chopped green chilies, drained and finely chopped	4 oz.	114 mL

Combine all 7 ingredients in medium bowl. Mix well. Chill for at least 2 hours. Makes 2 1/2 cups (625 mL).

2 tbsp. (30 mL): 13 Calories; 0.7 g Total Fat; 67 mg Sodium; trace Protein; 2 g Carbohydrate; trace Dietary Fiber

Pictured on page 17.

SALSA

You will find this type of sauce always on a Mexican table. It can be made as hot as you like. Serve as a sauce or a dip for corn chips.

Canned tomatoes	2 x 14 oz.	2 x 398 mL
Green pepper, chopped	1	1
Chopped onion	1/2 cup	125 mL
Garlic powder (or 1 clove, minced)	1/4 tsp.	1 mL
Salt	1/4 tsp.	1 mL
Canned pickled jalapeño pepper slices, drained (or more)	4	4

Put all 6 ingredients into blender. Process until smooth. Pour into medium saucepan. Bring to a boil. Simmer slowly for 10 minutes. Cool and pour into container. Makes 3 cups (750 mL).

2 tbsp. (30 mL): 9 Calories; 0.1 g Total Fat; 92 mg Sodium; trace Protein; 2 g Carbohydrate; trace Dietary Fiber

OVEN HOT DIP

Lots of red, green and orange showing. Serve with tortilla chips. This may be assembled and refrigerated until ready to heat and serve.

Cream cheese, softened	8 oz.	250 g
Commercial pizza sauce	1/2 cup	125 mL
Dried whole oregano	1/2 tsp.	2 mL
Garlic powder	1/4 tsp.	1 mL
Dried sweet basil	1/4 tsp.	1 mL
Onion powder	1/4 tsp.	1 mL
Chili powder (optional)	1/2-1 tsp.	2-5 mL
Finely chopped red pepper	1/2 cup	125 mL
Finely chopped green pepper	1/2 cup	125 mL
Sliced green onion	1/4 cup	60 mL
Grated sharp Cheddar cheese	1/2 cup	125 mL
Grated mozzarella cheese	1/2 cup	125 mL

Mix first 7 ingredients well in small bowl. Turn into ungreased 9 inch (22 cm) glass pie plate. Spread evenly.

Sprinkle with red pepper, green pepper, green onion, Cheddar cheese and mozzarella cheese. May be chilled at this point. Bake in 350°F (175°C) oven for 20 minutes. Makes about 3 cups (750 mL).

2 tbsp. (30 mL): 62 Calories; 5.2 g Total Fat; 80 mg Sodium; 2 g Protein; 2 g Carbohydrate; trace Dietary Fiber

---

Soften cream cheese by leaving it on the counter for several hours to bring it to room temperature. If using a microwave, place cream cheese on a microwave-safe plate and heat on very low (10%) for one-minute intervals to soften. Avoid melting.

crab dips

Crab is such a gourmet treat and goes far when used in these dips. Choose which version you want to serve—a cold dip or a hot dip.

★★★★★ ★★★★★

Canned crabmeat, drained and cartilage removed	4.2 oz.	120 g
Lemon juice	1/4 cup	60 mL
Cream cheese, softened	4 oz.	125 g
Cream (or milk)	2 tbsp.	30 mL
Salad dressing (or mayonnaise)	2 tbsp.	30 mL
Onion salt	1/4 tsp.	1 mL
Worcestershire sauce	1 tsp.	5 mL
Garlic powder	1/4 tsp.	0.5 mL
Cayenne pepper	1/4 tsp.	0.5 mL

Combine crabmeat and lemon juice in small bowl. Stir together well. Allow to marinate for 30 minutes. Drain.

Mash cream cheese and cream together in medium bowl. Add mayonnaise, onion salt and Worcestershire sauce. Add garlic powder being careful not to add too much so as to overpower the crabmeat flavor. Add cayenne pepper and beat together well. Stir in crabmeat. Add more cream if needed. Chill. Makes 1 1/2 cups (375 mL).

2 tbsp. (30 mL): 59 Calories; 5 g Total Fat; 149 mg Sodium; 2 g Protein; 1 g Carbohydrate; trace Dietary Fiber

CRAB CURRY DIP: Add 1/2 tsp. (2 mL) curry powder.

Canned crabmeat, drained and cartilage removed	5 oz.	142 g
Low-fat cottage cheese	1 cup	250 mL
Prepared horseradish	1/2 tsp.	2 mL
Salt	1/4 tsp.	1 mL
Skim milk	1 tbsp.	15 mL
Hard margarine (or butter), softened	1/4 cup	60 mL
Onion powder	1/4 tsp.	1 mL
Sliced almonds, toasted (see Note)	1/4 cup	60 mL

Combine first 7 ingredients in blender. Process until smooth. May be beaten in medium bowl instead of blender. Add more horseradish to taste. Turn into ungreased 1 quart (1 L) casserole dish. Smooth top.

Sprinkle almonds over crabmeat. Bake in 375°F (190°C) oven for about 20 minutes until hot. Makes 2 1/8 cups (530 mL).

Note: To toast almonds, place on baking sheet. Bake in 375°F (190°C) oven for 4 to 6 minutes until browned.

2 tbsp. (30 mL): 50 Calories; 18 g Total Fat; 184 mg Sodium; 2 g Protein; trace Carbohydrate; trace Dietary Fiber

SIMPLE SHRIMP DIP

Lots of flavor for dipping. Serve in dip bowl surrounded with your favorite chips and crackers. Also delicious with raw vegetables.

Sour cream	2 cups	500 mL
Chili sauce (or ketchup)	¼ cup	60 mL
Canned small (or broken) shrimp, drained and mashed	4 oz.	113 g
Lemon juice	½ tsp.	2 mL
Worcestershire sauce	½ tsp.	2 mL
Minced onion	1 tsp.	5 mL
Beef bouillon powder	½ tsp.	2 mL

Combine all 7 ingredients in medium bowl. Mash or beat together well. Serve chilled with chips and assorted crackers. Makes 2½ cups (625 mL).

2 tbsp. (30 mL): 45 Calories; 3.4 g Total Fat; 82 mg Sodium; 2 g Protein; 2 g Carbohydrate; trace Dietary Fiber

FAVORITE CLAM DIP

The name says it all. It's mild but always popular.

Cream cheese, softened	8 oz.	250 g
Canned minced clams, drained, liquid reserved	2 x 5 oz.	2 x 142 g
Lemon juice	1 tbsp.	15 mL
Worcestershire sauce	1 tsp.	5 mL
Onion salt	¼ tsp.	1 mL
Onion powder	¼ tsp.	1 mL
Reserved clam liquid (as needed)	5 tbsp.	75 mL

Beat first 6 ingredients together in medium bowl.

Add bit of reserved liquid, small amount at a time, until mixture is of dipping consistency. Makes 2½ cups (625 mL).

2 tbsp. (30 mL): 55 Calories; 4.4 g Total Fat; 96 mg Sodium; 3 g Protein; 1 g Carbohydrate; 0 g Dietary Fiber

SHRIMP DIP

The addition of Cheddar cheese makes this colorful. Just a faint hint of dill.

Finely grated mild Cheddar cheese	1 cup	250 mL
Salad dressing (or mayonnaise)	⅓ cup	75 mL
Sour cream	3 tbsp.	50 mL
Onion flakes	1 tbsp.	15 mL
Lemon juice	1 tsp.	5 mL
Paprika	¼ tsp.	1 mL
Dill weed	¼ tsp.	1 mL
Canned broken shrimp, drained and mashed	4 oz.	113 g
Milk (if needed)		

Mix first 7 ingredients in medium bowl.

Add shrimp. Mash together adding bit of milk for dipping consistency. Makes 1¼ cups (300 mL).

2 tbsp. (30 mL): 105 Calories; 8.4 g Total Fat; 139 mg Sodium; 5 g Protein; 2 g Carbohydrate; trace Dietary Fiber

CHIP DIP

Make this the day you need it or make several days ahead. Serve with potato chips and raw vegetables.

Salad dressing (or mayonnaise)	1 cup	250 mL
Soy sauce	1 tsp.	5 mL
Onion powder	¼ tsp.	1 mL
Parsley flakes	½ tsp.	2 mL
Red wine vinegar	1 tsp.	5 mL
Ground ginger	¼ tsp.	1 mL
Milk	2 tbsp.	30 mL

Stir all 7 ingredients together in small bowl. Add bit more milk if needed. Chill. Makes 1 cup (250 mL).

2 tbsp. (30 mL): 150 Calories; 14.6 g Total Fat; 272 mg Sodium; trace Protein; 4 g Carbohydrate; trace Dietary Fiber

Pictured on page 35.

HOT CRAB DIP

Just the right amount of zip to this good dip.

Cream cheese, softened	8 oz.	250 g
White (or alcohol-free white) wine	1 tbsp.	15 mL
Salad dressing (or mayonnaise)	2 tbsp.	30 mL
Prepared mustard	½ tsp.	2 mL
Onion flakes	2 tsp.	10 mL
Seasoning salt	½ tsp.	2 mL
Canned crabmeat, drained and cartilage removed	4.2 oz.	120 g

Place first 6 ingredients in small bowl. Beat together until smooth. Turn into double boiler.

Fold crabmeat into mixture using spatula. Heat over simmering water. Makes 1⅔ cups (400 mL).

2 tbsp. (30 mL): 82 Calories; 7.4 g Total Fat; 184 mg Sodium; 3 g Protein; 1 g Carbohydrate; trace Dietary Fiber

HOT BROCCOLI DIP

The melted cheese makes this a winning combination.

Hard margarine (or butter)	2 tbsp.	30 mL
Chopped onion	1 cup	250 mL
Chopped celery	1 cup	250 mL
Frozen chopped broccoli	10 oz.	300 g
Water, to cover		
Condensed cream of mushroom soup	10 oz.	284 mL
Salt	½ tsp.	2 mL
Garlic powder	¼ tsp.	1 mL
Worcestershire sauce	1 tsp.	5 mL
Cayenne pepper	¼ tsp.	1 mL
Grated sharp Cheddar cheese	1½ cups	375 mL

Melt margarine over low in large saucepan. Add onion and celery. Sauté until soft.

Cook broccoli in water in medium saucepan. Drain. Add to onion mixture. Stir together.

Add next 5 ingredients. Heat, stirring often, until mixture starts to simmer.

Add cheese. Stir until cheese is melted. Turn into chafing dish. Makes 3 cups (750 mL).

2 tbsp. (30 mL): 56 Calories; 4.3 g Total Fat; 215 mg Sodium; 2 g Protein; 2 g Carbohydrate; 1 g Dietary Fiber

BLACK BEAN DIP

A darkish dip with cheese sprinkled over top. Cider vinegar gives it a good tang. Serve with tortilla chips, corn chips or raw vegetables.

Canned black beans, drained	**19 oz.**	**540 mL**
Cider vinegar	**2 tsp.**	**10 mL**
Salt	**¹/₂ tsp.**	**2 mL**
Pepper	**¹/₈ tsp.**	**0.5 mL**
Garlic powder	**¹/₄ tsp.**	**1 mL**
Onion powder	**¹/₄ tsp.**	**1 mL**
Hot pepper sauce (optional)	**¹/₄-¹/₂ tsp.**	**1-2 mL**
TOPPING		
Grated medium Cheddar cheese	**¹/₄ cup**	**60 mL**
Ground walnuts	**1 tbsp.**	**15 mL**

Mash beans together well with fork on plate. Turn into small bowl.

Add next 6 ingredients. Stir together. Transfer to serving dish.

Topping: Sprinkle cheese and walnuts over top. Chill until needed. Makes 1¹/₃ cups (325 mL).

2 tbsp. (30 mL): 71 Calories; 1.5 g Total Fat; 254 mg Sodium; 5 g Protein; 10 g Carbohydrate; 2 g Dietary Fiber

Pictured on page 17.

DEVIL'S DIP

Serve this special dip hot from the oven and watch it disappear. Just the right nip. Serve with thin wheat crackers, tortilla chips or other crackers.

Cream cheese, softened	**8 oz.**	**250 g**
Sour cream	**1 cup**	**250 mL**
Canned jalapeño bean dip	**10¹/₂ oz.**	**298 g**
Drops hot pepper sauce	**10**	**10**
Dried chives	**3 tbsp.**	**50 mL**
Parsley flakes	**2 tsp.**	**10 mL**
Chili powder, to cover	**1 tsp.**	**5 mL**
Grated Monterey Jack cheese	**1¹/₂ cups**	**375 mL**
Grated medium Cheddar cheese	**1¹/₂ cups**	**375 mL**
Chili powder, sprinkle		

Mix first 6 ingredients in medium bowl. Spread in ungreased 9 x 13 inch (22 x 33 cm) pan.

Sprinkle chili powder over top, adding more if necessary to cover. Add layer of Monterey Jack cheese, then layer of Cheddar cheese. Sprinkle with chili powder. Bake in 350°F (175°C) oven for about 20 minutes or for 40 minutes for a crispy effect. Makes 4 cups (1 L).

2 tbsp. (30 mL): 87 Calories; 7.1 g Total Fat; 140 mg Sodium; 4 g Protein; 2 g Carbohydrate; trace Dietary Fiber

Variation: For a double devil's dip, stir 2 tbsp. (30 mL) chili powder into the first 6 ingredients.

Most taco and tortilla chips don't keep well past two months, even when left unopened. Aged chips take on a stale, musty odor and flavor. For this reason try to avoid buying in quantity if you don't plan to eat them right away.

TACO DIP

Always popular.

Canned jalapeño bean dip	10¹/₂ oz.	298 g
Avocados, peeled and mashed	3	3
Lemon juice	1 tsp.	5 mL
Garlic salt (or garlic powder)	1 tsp.	5 mL
Sour cream	1 cup	250 mL
Envelope taco seasoning mix	1 x 1¹/₄ oz.	1 x 35 g
Grated Monterey Jack cheese	1 cup	250 mL
Grated medium Cheddar cheese	1 cup	250 mL
Ripe large tomatoes, diced and drained on paper towels	2	2
Green onions, thinly sliced	4	4

Spread bean dip in ungreased 12 inch (30 cm) pizza pan or 10 inch (25 cm) quiche dish.

Mix avocado, lemon juice and garlic salt. Spread over bean dip.

Stir sour cream and seasoning mix together in small bowl. Spread over avocado layer.

Sprinkle with Monterey Jack cheese, Cheddar cheese, tomato and green onion. Makes 4 cups (1 L).

2 tbsp. (30 mL): 56 Calories; 3.5 g Total Fat; 257 mg Sodium; 3 g Protein; 4 g Carbohydrate; 1 g Dietary Fiber

Pictured on page 17.

SPREADING FOREST FIRE

This is a quick bean dip. A natural for corn chips and tortilla chips.

Canned beans in tomato sauce, drained and mashed	14 oz.	398 mL
Grated sharp Cheddar cheese	1 cup	250 mL
Hard margarine (or butter)	¹/₂ cup	125 mL
Very finely chopped onion	¹/₂ cup	125 mL
Garlic powder	¹/₄ tsp.	1 mL
Salt	¹/₄ tsp.	1 mL
Pepper	¹/₈ tsp.	0.5 mL
Hot pepper sauce (see Note)	¹/₂ tsp.	2 mL

Put all 8 ingredients into medium saucepan. Heat and stir until cheese and margarine are melted. Serve warm. Makes 3 cups (750 mL).

2 tbsp. (30 mL): 71 Calories; 5.6 g Total Fat; 171 mg Sodium; 2 g Protein; 4 g Carbohydrate; 1 g Dietary Fiber

Note: A few slices of jalapeño peppers, ground, may be substituted for the hot pepper sauce. Then you really will have a fire!

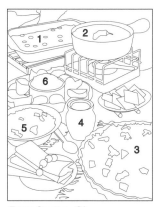

1. Mexican Bean Dip, page 9
2. Chili Con Queso, page 8
3. Taco Dip, page 16
4. Jalapeño Jelly, page 73
5. Salsa Cruda, page 11
6. Black Bean Dip, page 15

Props Courtesy Of:
Chintz & Company, Creations By Design, Eaton's, Scona Clayworks, Stokes

GARBANZO PÂTÉ

A soft pâté. Serve with crackers and ripe olives.

Cooking oil	2 tbsp.	30 mL
Chopped onion	1 cup	250 mL
Small green pepper, chopped	1	1
Chopped celery	1/3 cup	75 mL
Canned chick peas (garbanzo beans), drained	14 oz.	398 mL
Lemon juice	4 tsp.	20 mL
Dried whole oregano	1 tsp.	5 mL
Garlic powder	1/4 tsp.	1 mL
Salt	1/2 tsp.	2 mL
Pepper	1/8 tsp.	0.5 mL
Ripe pitted olives, for garnish		

Heat cooking oil in medium frying pan. Add onion, green pepper and celery. Sauté for 10 to 15 minutes until soft.

Combine next 6 ingredients in blender or food processor. Add onion mixture. Process until smooth. Garnish with ripe olives. Makes 1¾ cups (425 mL).

2 tbsp. (30 mL): 47 Calories; 2.3 g Total Fat; 131 mg Sodium; 1 g Protein; 6 g Carbohydrate; 1 g Dietary Fiber

DILL DIP

A handy snack. Set out dip and chips for guests to help themselves. Also good as a dip for raw vegetables.

Salad dressing (or mayonnaise)	1 cup	250 mL
Sour cream	1 cup	250 mL
Parsley flakes	1 tsp.	5 mL
Dill weed	1 tsp.	5 mL
Onion powder	1/2 tsp.	2 mL
Celery salt	1/2 tsp.	2 mL

Mix all 6 ingredients in small bowl. Chill until needed. Makes 2 cups (500 mL).

2 tbsp. (30 mL): 96 Calories; 9.3 g Total Fat; 121 mg Sodium; 1 g Protein; 3 g Carbohydrate; trace Dietary Fiber

Most dips improve in flavor when prepared in advance and left to sit in the refrigerator. Flavors blend and dried spices and herbs soften, becoming more pungent. Cover bowl with lid or plastic wrap.

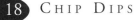

Fish & Seafood Dips

Here are some irresistible dips for seafood lovers to explore. Try *Curried Tartar Sauce* the next time you plan a seafood night with friends and family. *Shrimp's Delight* is a scrumptious alternative to traditional cocktail sauce, and *Cheesy Artichoke Fondue* is a rich and soothing meal to share with good friends.

CHEESY ARTICHOKE FONDUE

Try this and the variation. Make ahead and reheat on stove top when ready to fondue. Add a bit of milk to thin if needed.

Hard margarine (or butter)	3 tbsp.	50 mL
All-purpose flour	3 tbsp.	50 mL
Milk	1¼ cups	300 mL
Canned artichoke hearts, drained and chopped	14 oz.	398 mL
Sherry (or alcohol-free sherry)	¼ cup	60 mL
Herbed cream cheese	4 oz.	125 g
Bacon slices, cooked crisp and crumbled	2	2
Pepper, sprinkle		

Melt margarine over low in medium saucepan. Mix in flour. Stir in milk until boiling and thickened.

Add remaining 5 ingredients. Stir until cheese is melted. Pour into fondue pot. Keep warm over low flame. Makes 2 cups (500 mL).

2 tbsp. (30 mL): 76 Calories; 5.8 g Total Fat; 111 mg Sodium; 2 g Protein; 4 g Carbohydrate; 1 g Dietary Fiber

Variation: Omit herbed cream cheese. Add 1 cup (250 mL) grated Swiss cheese or sharp Cheddar cheese.

CURRIED MAYONNAISE

This is so good served with fish. Make this the day before it is to be used so flavors blend.

Salad dressing (or mayonnaise)	1 cup	250 mL
White vinegar	1 tbsp.	15 mL
Brown sugar, packed	1 tbsp.	15 mL
Prepared mustard	1 tsp.	5 mL
Curry powder	1 tsp.	5 mL

Combine all 5 ingredients in jar. Stir together well. Chill. Makes generous 1 cup (250 mL).

2 tbsp. (30 mL): 155 Calories; 14.6 g Total Fat; 196 mg Sodium; trace Protein; 6 g Carbohydrate; trace Dietary Fiber

SHRIMP'S DELIGHT

A wonderful seafood dip. Serve with cold cooked large shrimp with tails intact.

Chili sauce	1 cup	250 mL
Salad dressing (or mayonnaise)	½ cup	125 mL
Sweet pickle relish	¼ cup	60 mL
Prepared horseradish	1 tsp.	5 mL
Worcestershire sauce	1 tsp.	5 mL

Stir all 5 ingredients together in small bowl. Makes 1¾ cups (425 mL).

2 tbsp. (30 mL): 67 Calories; 4.2 g Total Fat; 341 mg Sodium; 1 g Protein; 7 g Carbohydrate; 1 g Dietary Fiber

SHRIMP COCKTAIL DIP

A family favorite to begin a favorite family meal.

Chili sauce	¾ cup	175 mL
Lemon juice	2 tsp.	10 mL
Worcestershire sauce	¼-1 tsp.	1-5 mL
Onion powder	½ tsp.	2 mL
Salt	¼ tsp.	1 mL
Peeled and finely diced apple	½ cup	125 mL
Finely chopped celery	¼ cup	60 mL

Mix all 7 ingredients in small bowl, using smallest amount of Worcestershire sauce. Add to taste. Makes 1½ cups (375 mL).

2 tbsp. (30 mL): 22 Calories; 0.1 g Total Fat; 290 mg Sodium; trace Protein; 5 g Carbohydrate; 1 g Dietary Fiber

CURRIED TARTAR SAUCE

Only three ingredients. Couldn't get any easier!

Salad dressing (or mayonnaise)	1 cup	250 mL
Sweet pickle relish	2 tbsp.	30 mL
Curry powder	¼ tsp.	1 mL

Mix all 3 ingredients in small bowl. Makes 1 cup (250 mL).

2 tbsp. (30 mL): 151 Calories; 14.6 g Total Fat; 202 mg Sodium; trace Protein; 5 g Carbohydrate; trace Dietary Fiber

Fruit Dips

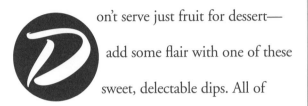

on't serve just fruit for dessert—

add some flair with one of these

sweet, delectable dips. All of

these fruit dips are simple and quick to prepare.

Save time by making them a day or two in

advance and refrigerating until needed.

CUPID'S DIP

When the ancient Romans fed grapes to their loved ones, they didn't have a dip like this to enjoy!

Granulated sugar	**¼ cup**	**60 mL**
Cornstarch	**¼ cup**	**60 mL**
Salt	**¼ tsp.**	**1 mL**
Pineapple juice	**1 cup**	**250 mL**
Prepared orange juice	**¼ cup**	**60 mL**
Lemon juice	**2 tbsp.**	**30 mL**
Large eggs, fork-beaten	**2**	**2**
Grenadine syrup	**2 tbsp.**	**30 mL**
Cream cheese, softened	**8 oz.**	**250 g**

Mix sugar, cornstarch and salt in medium saucepan.

Add pineapple, orange and lemon juices. Heat and stir in eggs and grenadine until mixture is boiling and thickened.

Add cream cheese in small pieces. Whisk or beat together until melted and smooth. Chill. Makes 3 cups (750 mL).

2 tbsp. (30 mL): 66 Calories; 3.9 g Total Fat; 63 mg Sodium; 1 g Protein; 7 g Carbohydrate; trace Dietary Fiber

DELUXE CHOCOLATE FONDUE SAUCE

Just a hint of liqueur flavor. Place dippers in freezer for about 30 minutes to chill if desired. The chocolate will solidify slightly on contact.

Good quality milk chocolate, cut up	8 oz.	250 g
Bittersweet chocolate baking squares, broken up	4 x 1 oz.	4 x 28 g
Whipping cream	1 cup	250 mL
Tia Maria liqueur (or Cognac)	2 tbsp.	30 mL

Combine all 4 ingredients in top of double boiler. Heat, stirring often, until chocolate is melted and blended. Pour into chocolate fondue pot. Keep warm over low flame. Makes 1⅓ cups (325 mL).

2 tbsp. (30 mL): 246 Calories; 20.2 g Total Fat; 27 mg Sodium; 3 g Protein; 17 g Carbohydrate; 2 g Dietary Fiber

CHOCOLATE FONDUE SAUCE

Only three ingredients in this smooth-as-satin topping. Serve hot or cold. Also makes a good fondue dip.

Evaporated milk	1 cup	250 mL
Semisweet chocolate chips	1½ cups	375 mL
Vanilla	1 tsp.	5 mL

Combine milk, chocolate chips and vanilla in small saucepan. Cook over low until chocolate chips combine when stirred. Remove from heat. Makes 1⅔ cups (400 mL).

2 tbsp. (30 mL): 100 Calories; 6.1 g Total Fat; 24 mg Sodium; 2 g Protein; 11 g Carbohydrate; 1 g Dietary Fiber

Pictured on front cover.

Most fruits make excellent dessert dippers for fondue or other sweet dips. Try honeydew melon, cantaloupe, watermelon, banana, apples, oranges, grapes, strawberries, peaches, nectarines, pineapple (fresh or canned), papaya, mango and kiwifruit. Other fun dippers include marshmallows, cubes of pound cake or brownies, shortbread cookies, and even maraschino cherries. Pretzels and meringues are great served with chocolate dips. If using canned fruit, drain well, then carefully pat with a paper towel.

CHOCOLATE DIP

Great for dipping barbecued fruit, cake, marshmallows, anything.

Semisweet chocolate baking squares	8	8
Light cream (half-and-half)	⅔ cup	150 mL
Rum flavoring (optional)	1 tsp.	5 mL

Combine all 3 ingredients in top of double boiler. Heat, stirring often, until chocolate is melted. Makes about 1 cup (250 mL).

2 tbsp. (30 mL): 160 Calories; 11.7 g Total Fat; 12 mg Sodium; 2 g Protein; 16 g Carbohydrate; 2 g Dietary Fiber

CARAMEL FONDUE SAUCE

Perfect consistency for dipping. Unwrap the caramels and prepare the dippers before dinner, or make the sauce and freeze. Reheat just before you are ready to sit down for dessert.

Light cream (half-and-half)	⅔ cup	150 mL
Chewy caramel candies (about 53)	1 lb.	454 g

Place cream and caramels in top of double boiler. Heat, stirring constantly, until melted and smooth. Pour into fondue pot. Keep warm over low flame. Makes 1¾ cups (425 mL).

2 tbsp. (30 mL): 138 Calories; 4.4 g Total Fat; 87 mg Sodium; 2 g Protein; 24 g Carbohydrate; 0 g Dietary Fiber

Variation: Use chocolate caramels or a mixture of both.

CHEESE FONDUE SAUCE

Keep heat very low to avoid cheese going stringy. Use this for dipping chunks of French bread, apple slices, seedless grapes or stuffed green olives.

Condensed Cheddar cheese soup	10 oz.	284 mL
Grated farmer's (or Cheddar) cheese	1 cup	250 mL
Grated Parmesan cheese	½ cup	125 mL
Green onions, finely chopped	2	2
Garlic powder	⅛ tsp.	0.5 mL
Hot pepper sauce, dash		

Measure all 6 ingredients into medium saucepan. Heat over low, stirring often, until melted and hot. Transfer to fondue pot. If sauce gets too thick for dipping, dilute with white wine, beer or fruit juice. Makes 2½ cups (625 mL).

2 tbsp. (30 mL): 69 Calories; 4.9 g Total Fat; 258 mg Sodium; 5 g Protein; 2 g Carbohydrate; trace Dietary Fiber

---

Serve fruit chunks with colored toothpicks or cocktail picks. Use fondue forks or bamboo skewers for hot fondue dips. Leave green leafy ends on strawberries for a natural "handle."

fruit dips

These dips each offer a unique taste sensation from tropical to rum-flavored. Please pass the fruit plate!

★★★★★

Low-fat (or regular) sour cream	1 cup	250 mL
Brown sugar, packed	⅓ cup	75 mL
Coconut (or oatmeal) cookies, finely crushed	3	3

Place all 3 ingredients in small bowl. Mix. Cover. Chill for several hours or overnight to blend flavors. Makes generous 1 cup (250 mL).

2 tbsp. (30 mL): 97 Calories; 3.8 g Total Fat; 18 mg Sodium; 1 g Protein; 15 g Carbohydrate; trace Dietary Fiber

★★★★★

Cream cheese, softened	8 oz.	250 mL
Marshmallow cream	½ cup	125 mL
Frozen concentrated orange juice	2 tsp.	10 mL
Grated orange peel	1 tsp.	5 mL

Combine all 4 ingredients in small bowl. Beat together until smooth. Makes 1 cup (250 mL).

2 tbsp. (30 mL): 153 Calories; 10.5 g Total Fat; 95 mg Sodium; 3 g Protein; 13 g Carbohydrate; trace Dietary Fiber

★★★★★

Frozen whipped topping (in a tub), thawed	2 cups	500 mL
Brown sugar, packed	¼ cup	60 mL
Ground cinnamon	¼ tsp.	1 mL

Stir whipped topping, brown sugar and cinnamon together in small bowl. Makes 2 cups (500 mL).

2 tbsp. (30 mL): 43 Calories; 2.4 g Total Fat; 3 mg Sodium; trace Protein; 6 g Carbohydrate; trace Dietary Fiber

Pictured on page 89.

★★★★★

Sour cream	1½ cups	375 mL
Salad dressing (or mayonnaise)	¼ cup	60 mL
Brown sugar, packed	¼ cup	60 mL
Chopped raisins	⅓ cup	75 mL
Rum flavoring	¼ tsp.	1 mL

Combine all 5 ingredients in medium bowl. Stir together well. Chill. Makes 2 cups (500 mL).

2 tbsp. (30 mL): 75 Calories; 4.9 g Total Fat; 34 mg Sodium; 1 g Protein; 8 g Carbohydrate; trace Dietary Fiber

EASY FRUIT DIP

You can whip this up in no time.

Plain yogurt	**1 cup**	**250 mL**
Icing (confectioner's) sugar	**3 tbsp.**	**50 mL**
Grated lemon peel	**½ tsp.**	**2 mL**

Combine all 3 ingredients in small bowl. Stir together well. Makes 1 cup (250 mL).

2 tbsp. (30 mL): 29 Calories; 0.5 g Total Fat; 22 mg Sodium; 2 g Protein; 5 g Carbohydrate; trace Dietary Fiber

---

When fruit is being served with a dip, chances are it will sit at room temperature for a prolonged period of time. Some fruits, such as apples, bananas and peaches will turn brown. To avoid this, brush pieces with lemon juice and keep chilled until you are ready to serve.

fruit toppings

A simple fruit dessert can easily be enhanced with these flavorful toppings.

★★★★★

Cream cheese, softened	**4 oz.**	**125 g**
Sour cream	**¼ cup**	**60 mL**
Prepared orange juice	**2 tbsp.**	**30 mL**
Icing (confectioner's) sugar	**2 tbsp.**	**30 mL**
Lemon juice	**1 tsp.**	**5 mL**

Combine cream cheese and sour cream in small bowl. Add orange juice, icing sugar and lemon juice. Beat together well. Makes scant 1 cup (250 mL).

2 tbsp. (30 mL): 72 Calories; 6.3 g Total Fat; 48 mg Sodium; 1 g Protein; 3 g Carbohydrate; trace Dietary Fiber

★★★★★

Envelope dessert topping, prepared according to package directions (see Note)	**1**	**1**
Raspberry-flavored yogurt	**1 cup**	**250 mL**

Stir dessert topping and yogurt together in medium bowl. Makes 3 cups (750 mL).

2 tbsp. (30 mL): 20 Calories; 0.8 g Total Fat; 7 mg Sodium; trace Protein; 3 g Carbohydrate; 0 g Dietary Fiber

Note: 1 cup (250 mL) whipping cream, whipped, can be substituted for dessert topping.

FRUIT FROSTING

A dream dip that makes up quickly.

Cream cheese, softened	8 oz.	250 g
Jar marshmallow cream	7 oz.	200 g
Milk	2 tbsp.	30 mL
Lemon juice	⅛ tsp.	0.5 mL

Beat all 4 ingredients together in medium bowl. Makes about 2 cups (500 mL).

2 tbsp. (30 mL): 91 Calories; 5.3 g Total Fat; 51 mg Sodium; 1 g Protein; 10 g Carbohydrate; 0 g Dietary Fiber

SPICY DIP

This cinnamon-flavored dip is just right for apples and other fruit.

Sour cream	1 cup	250 mL
Brown sugar, packed	2 tbsp.	30 mL
Ground cinnamon	⅛ tsp.	0.5 mL
Brandy flavoring	1 tsp.	5 mL

Stir all 4 ingredients together in small bowl. Makes 1 cup (250 mL).

2 tbsp. (30 mL): 57 Calories; 4.1 g Total Fat; 14 mg Sodium; 1 g Protein; 5 g Carbohydrate; trace Dietary Fiber

ORANGE FRUIT DIP

Serve with a platter of assorted fresh fruits.

Sour cream	1 cup	250 mL
Brown sugar, packed	1 tbsp.	15 mL
Grand Marnier (or other orange-flavored liqueur), see Note	1 tbsp.	15 mL

Stir all 3 ingredients together in small bowl. Makes 1 cup (250 mL).

2 tbsp. (30 mL): 55 Calories; 4.1 g Total Fat; 13 mg Sodium; 1 g Protein; 3 g Carbohydrate; trace Dietary Fiber

Note: You can substitute more brown sugar for the liqueur.

Be creative when cutting your fruit. Use a melon baller for perfect round shapes, and cut others into wedges or triangles. Arrange on your platter using a variety of contrasting colors and textures.

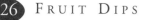

STRAWBERRY DIP

A pretty pink topping for fruit and cake.

Fresh strawberries, cut up	1 cup	250 mL
Granulated sugar	¼ cup	60 mL
Creamed cottage cheese, drained	⅓ cup	75 mL
Sour cream	⅓ cup	75 mL

Combine strawberries and sugar in small bowl. Stir together. Let stand for 10 minutes, stirring twice. Drain in sieve. Place berry mixture in blender.

Add cottage cheese and sour cream. Process until smooth. Turn into small bowl. Chill. Makes 1½ cups (375 mL).

2 tbsp. (30 mL): 34 Calories; 1 g Total Fat; 29 mg Sodium; 1 g Protein; 6 g Carbohydrate; trace Dietary Fiber

ORANGE COCONUT FRUIT DIP

Pale yellow in color. Goes well with fruit.

Creamed cottage cheese	2 cups	500 mL
Sour cream	¼ cup	60 mL
Frozen concentrated orange juice	2 tbsp.	30 mL
Granulated sugar	2 tbsp.	30 mL
Fine or medium unsweetened coconut	¼ cup	60 mL

Measure first 4 ingredients into blender. Process until smooth. Turn into small bowl.

Stir in coconut. Makes 1½ cups (375 mL).

2 tbsp. (30 mL): 61 Calories; 2.3 g Total Fat; 163 mg Sodium; 5 g Protein; 5 g Carbohydrate; trace Dietary Fiber

CARAMEL FRUIT DIP

Make a good supply. It vanishes in no time.

Sour cream	1 cup	250 mL
Brown sugar, packed	1 tbsp.	15 mL
Kahlua (see Note)	1 tbsp.	15 mL

Stir all 3 ingredients together in small bowl. Makes 1 cup (250 mL).

2 tbsp. (30 mL): 57 Calories; 4.1 g Total Fat; 13 mg Sodium; 1 g Protein; 4 g Carbohydrate; trace Dietary Fiber

CHEESY DIP

Serve with fruit of your choice. Has a slight hint of sherry.

Finely grated medium Cheddar cheese	1 cup	250 mL
Cream cheese, softened	8 oz.	250 g
Milk	3 tbsp.	50 mL
Sherry (or alcohol-free sherry)	1 tbsp.	15 mL
Finely grated medium Cheddar cheese	1 tbsp.	15 mL

Beat first 4 ingredients together in small bowl. Place in serving bowl.

Top with second amount of Cheddar cheese. Makes 2 cups (500 mL).

2 tbsp. (30 mL): 85 Calories; 7.8 g Total Fat; 93 mg Sodium; 3 g Protein; 1 g Carbohydrate; 0 g Dietary Fiber

───────

A fruit and dip dessert is best served after a light, savory main course. This dessert also works well at a stand-up afternoon gathering or evening cocktail party.

CRANBERRY DIP

A pretty Christmas dip.

Jellied cranberry	14 oz.	398 mL
Lemon juice	2 tsp.	10 mL
Prepared mustard	½ tsp.	2 mL
Granulated sugar	2 tbsp.	30 mL

Mix all 4 ingredients well in small bowl. Makes 1½ cups (375 mL).

2 tbsp. (30 mL): 64 Calories; 0.1 g Total Fat; 14 mg Sodium; trace Protein; 17 g Carbohydrate; trace Dietary Fiber

PEANUT BUTTER DIP

Very few ingredients. Very simple. Very good.

Smooth peanut butter	1 cup	250 mL
Vanilla ice cream	2 cups	500 mL

Stir peanut butter and ice cream together in medium bowl until ice cream is melted and blended in. Makes 2½ cups (625 mL).

2 tbsp. (30 mL): 117 Calories; 8.7 g Total Fat; 80 mg Sodium; 4 g Protein; 8 g Carbohydrate; 1 g Dietary Fiber

Variation: Dip fruit into Peanut Butter Dip then into 1 cup (250 mL) finely chopped or ground peanuts. Crunch away!

Vegetable Dips

repare these dips ahead of time so that flavors can blend together. Here is a selection of dips and dunks that use cream cheese, salad dressings or sour cream as their base ingredient. For an eye-catching presentation, serve any of these dips in an edible bread bowl or scooped out squash shells surrounded by your favorite vegetables.

BEST VEGETABLE DIP

Make up this large recipe, use half and freeze half. Ready to take with you or to use at a moment's notice. A sweeter than usual vegetable dip.

Cream cheese, softened	8 oz.	250 g
Corn syrup	½ cup	125 mL
Granulated sugar	½ cup	125 mL
Cooking oil	1 cup	250 mL
White vinegar	¼ cup	60 mL
Minced onion flakes (or use ¾ cup, 175 mL, minced fresh onion)	¼ cup	60 mL
Lemon juice	1 tbsp.	15 mL
Dry mustard	1 tsp.	5 mL
Celery seed	1 tsp.	5 mL
Salt	½ tsp.	2 mL
Paprika	¼ tsp.	1 mL

Put cream cheese, corn syrup and sugar into medium bowl. Beat together well. Add cooking oil and mix. Add remaining 7 ingredients. Beat together until blended. Chill. Makes 3 cups (750 mL).

2 tbsp. (30 mL): 158 Calories; 12.8 g Total Fat; 89 mg Sodium; 1 g Protein; 11 g Carbohydrate; trace Dietary Fiber

Vegetables that work well as dippers are broccoli and cauliflower florets, carrot chunks, whole mushrooms, cherry tomatoes, bell pepper strips/chunks (green, red, yellow and orange), cucumber chunks and asparagus tips. Cut up an assortment of vegetables the night before and store in individual plastic bags in the refrigerator. Fill your vegetable trays just before serving, and replenish as guests help themselves.

HUMMUS

HOOM-uhs has a bit of a lemony tang. Light in color, tasty and nutty in flavor. Can be served in bowl or on bed of lettuce.

Canned chick peas (garbanzo beans), drained and liquid reserved	19 oz.	540 mL
Lemon juice	¼ cup	60 mL
Tahini (sesame spread)	⅓ cup	75 mL
Garlic powder	½ tsp.	2 mL
Onion powder	¼ tsp.	1 mL
Salt	½ tsp.	2 mL
Pepper	⅛ tsp.	0.5 mL
Reserved chick pea liquid	6 tbsp.	100 mL

Pour chick peas and lemon juice into blender. Process until smooth.

Add tahini, garlic powder, onion powder, salt and pepper. Process to mix. Add reserved liquid as needed to thin so it is like soft whipped cream. Makes 2½ cups (575 mL).

2 tbsp. (30 mL): 55 Calories; 2.4 g Total Fat; 145 mg Sodium; 2 g Protein; 7 g Carbohydrate; 1 g Dietary Fiber

STICK DIP

A quick-to-make dip for a bag lunch that includes breadsticks, raw vegetables or crackers.

Sour cream	3 tbsp.	50 mL
Beef bouillon powder	½ tsp.	2 mL
Onion salt	¼ tsp.	1 mL

Put sour cream, bouillon powder and onion salt into small bowl. Mix well. Makes 3 tbsp. (50 mL).

2 tbsp. (30 mL): 48 Calories; 4.2 g Total Fat; 446 mg Sodium; 1 g Protein; 2 g Carbohydrate; trace Dietary Fiber

CURRY DIP

Indulge in this easy and speedy dip. Curry flavor is mild and adds to the good taste.

Salad dressing (or mayonnaise)	1 cup	250 mL
Grated onion	2 tsp.	10 mL
Prepared horseradish	2 tsp.	10 mL
Curry powder	1 tsp.	5 mL
Salt	1 tsp.	5 mL

Mix all 5 ingredients in small bowl. Makes about 1 cup (250 mL).

2 tbsp. (30 mL): 149 Calories; 14.6 g Total Fat; 513 mg Sodium; trace Protein; 4 g Carbohydrate; trace Dietary Fiber

TERIYAKI SESAME DIP

Serve warm as a fondue sauce for raw meat or cold as a dip for cooked meatballs or vegetables. Make up to one week in advance and keep chilled.

Low-sodium soy sauce	½ cup	125 mL
Garlic powder	¼ tsp.	1 mL
White wine (or apple juice)	¼ cup	60 mL
Brown sugar, packed	2 tbsp.	30 mL
Cornstarch	1 tbsp.	15 mL
Toasted sesame seed	2 tbsp.	30 mL

Combine soy sauce, garlic powder and white wine in small saucepan.

Stir brown sugar and cornstarch together in small bowl. Add to liquid mixture in saucepan, stirring frequently, until mixture is thickened and clear.

Add sesame seed. Makes ¾ cup (175 mL).

2 tbsp. (30 mL): 60 Calories; 1.5 g Total Fat; 835 mg Sodium; 3 g Protein; 8 g Carbohydrate; 1 g Dietary Fiber

CHILI HORSERADISH DIP

Orange-red with dark flecks of celery. Make ahead and refrigerate for up to one week.

Chili sauce	½ cup	125 mL
Prepared horseradish	¼ cup	60 mL
White vinegar	1 tbsp.	15 mL
Granulated sugar	1 tsp.	5 mL
Celery seed	1 tsp.	5 mL
Worcestershire sauce	1 tsp.	5 mL
Garlic salt	¼ tsp.	1 mL

Mix all 7 ingredients in small bowl. Chill for several hours so flavors can blend. Makes a generous ¾ cup (175 mL).

2 tbsp. (30 mL): 33 Calories; 0.2 g Total Fat; 384 mg Sodium; 1 g Protein; 8 g Carbohydrate; 2 g Dietary Fiber

Lightly steaming broccoli florets and asparagus tips for a vegetable tray will enhance their color and make them a bit easier to bite into. Steam vegetables over boiling water until their color brightens. Remove from saucepan and place in a bowl of ice water to stop further cooking.

spinach dips

This makes a large amount but don't be concerned, you'll need it. It's great.

Frozen chopped spinach, thawed and squeezed dry	10 oz.	300 g
Salad dressing (or mayonnaise)	1 cup	250 mL
Sour cream	1 cup	250 mL
Chopped onion	½ cup	125 mL
Envelope dry vegetable soup mix	1 × 1½ oz.	1 × 45 g
Canned water chestnuts, drained and chopped	8 oz.	227 mL

Place first 4 ingredients in blender. Process until smooth. Turn into medium bowl.

Stir in soup mix and water chestnuts. Cover. Chill for at least 2 hours. Makes 3¾ cups (925 mL).

2 tbsp. (30 mL): 64 Calories; 5.4 g Total Fat; 129 mg Sodium; 1 g Protein; 3 g Carbohydrate; trace Dietary Fiber

This makes a spectacular splash whether served in a bowl or a bread shell. It will vanish either way.

Frozen chopped spinach, thawed and squeezed dry	10 oz.	300 g
Sour cream	1 cup	250 mL
Salad dressing (or mayonnaise)	1 cup	250 mL
Chopped green onion	½ cup	125 mL
Parsley flakes	1 tsp.	5 mL
Lemon juice	1 tsp.	5 mL
Seasoning salt	½ tsp.	2 mL

Put spinach, sour cream and salad dressing into medium bowl. Stir together. Add green onion, parsley, lemon juice and seasoning salt. Mix. Chill. Heat before serving. Makes 3½ cups (875 mL).

2 tbsp. (30 mL): 57 Calories; 5.4 g Total Fat; 85 mg Sodium; 1 g Protein; 2 g Carbohydrate; trace Dietary Fiber

To make a unique serving bowl for any of the spinach dips or for King Artichoke Dip, page 7, use a round bread loaf (white, whole wheat, pumpernickel, sourdough or other). Cut top off about ¼ to ⅓ of the way down. Remove bread from inside, leaving shell about 1 inch (2.5 cm) thick. (Reserve bread chunks for dipping.) At this point you may fill the hollowed loaf with dip. You may need to double the recipe if the loaf is large. To serve heated, you may wrap the filled loaf in foil and place in 300°F (150°C) oven for two hours. The bread does tend to harden soon after cooling, however, so you may prefer to heat the dip in an ovenproof container, remove from oven and fill bread bowl with dip. To prevent bacteria from setting in, it's important to ensure that this dip does not sit out on a buffet table all afternoon. Of course, the best part of this appetizer is tearing up and munching the serving bowl when finished!

spinach dips

Lower in calories and fat than similar dips. Good flavor. This is good served warm or at room temperature.

Low-fat cottage cheese	1 cup	250 mL
Light salad dressing (or mayonnaise)	1 cup	250 mL
Lemon juice	2 tbsp.	30 mL
Chopped onion	1/3 cup	75 mL
Frozen chopped spinach, thawed and squeezed dry	10 oz.	300 g
Parsley flakes	2 tsp.	10 mL

Place first 4 ingredients in blender. Process until smooth. Turn into medium bowl.

Stir in spinach and parsley. Makes 2²/₃ cups (650 mL).

2 tbsp. (30 mL): 46 Calories; 3.1 g Total Fat; 145 mg Sodium; 2 g Protein; 3 g Carbohydrate; trace Dietary Fiber

This can be served with bread, crackers or fresh veggies.

Salad dressing (or mayonnaise)	1/2 cup	125 mL
Cream cheese, softened	2 x 8 oz.	2 x 250 g
Grated medium or sharp Cheddar cheese	1 cup	250 mL
Frozen chopped spinach, thawed and squeezed dry	10 oz.	300 g
Bacon slices, cooked crisp and crumbled	6	6
Finely chopped onion	1/4 cup	60 mL
Dill weed	2 tsp.	10 mL
Garlic powder (or 1 clove, minced)	1/4 tsp.	1 mL

Beat salad dressing and cream cheese together in small bowl until smooth. Stir in remaining 6 ingredients. Makes 3 cups (750 mL).

2 tbsp. (30 mL): 125 Calories; 11.8 g Total Fat; 149 mg Sodium; 3 g Protein; 2 g Carbohydrate; trace Dietary Fiber

Pictured on page 35.

Dried herbs have a stronger flavor than fresh herbs. When substituting dried for fresh herbs, or vice-versa, the approximate rule of thumb is: 1/4 tsp. (1 mL) finely ground dried herbs is equal to 2 tsp. (10 mL) chopped fresh herbs. When using dried crumbled herbs, 1 tsp. (5 mL) is equal to 2 tsp. (10 mL) chopped fresh herbs.

CLAM DIP

Mild in flavor. This recipe could be increased and served in a hollowed-out round bread loaf.

Cream cheese, softened	4 oz.	125 g
Canned minced clams, drained	5 oz.	142 g
Lemon juice	1 tsp.	5 mL
Garlic powder	¼ tsp.	1 mL
Onion salt	½ tsp.	2 mL
Worcestershire sauce	½ tsp.	2 mL
Milk	2 tbsp.	30 mL

Mix all 7 ingredients well in small bowl, adding enough milk to make dipping consistency. Chill. Makes generous 1 cup (250 mL).

2 tbsp. (30 mL): 70 Calories; 5.5 g Total Fat; 142 mg Sodium; 4 g Protein; 1 g Carbohydrate; trace Dietary Fiber

BACON CHEDDAR DIP

Everybody raves over this. Easy to spread or dip.

Salad dressing (or mayonnaise)	1 cup	250 mL
Buttermilk	1 cup	250 mL
Grated medium Cheddar cheese	1 cup	250 mL
Onion flakes	¼ cup	60 mL
Imitation bacon bits	⅓ cup	75 mL
Garlic salt	¾ tsp.	4 mL

Mix all 6 ingredients in medium bowl. Cover. Chill for 30 minutes. Makes 2⅓ cups (575 mL).

2 tbsp. (30 mL): 111 Calories; 8.7 g Total Fat; 297 mg Sodium; 3 g Protein; 6 g Carbohydrate; trace Dietary Fiber

1. Herb Dip, page 37
2. Cheese Roll, page 63
3. Spinach Dip, page 33
4. Chip Dip, page 14
5. Surprise Spread, page 88
6. Ham Spread, page 92
7. Egg Salad Spread, page 93

Props Courtesy Of:
Chintz & Company
Eaton's, Stokes

vegetable dips

It will take you less time to prepare these dips than to cut up your dippers!

★★★★★

Salad dressing (or mayonnaise)	2 cups	500 mL
Ketchup	3 tbsp.	50 mL
Worcestershire sauce	1 tsp.	5 mL
Garlic powder	½ tsp.	2 mL
Onion salt	½ tsp.	2 mL
Curry powder	½ tsp.	2 mL

Combine all 6 ingredients in small bowl. Stir well. A bit of milk may be added if too thick. Chill. Makes generous 2 cups (500 mL).

2 tbsp. (30 mL): 152 Calories; 14.6 g Total Fat; 308 mg Sodium; trace Protein; 5 g Carbohydrate; trace Dietary Fiber

★★★★★

Medium onion	½	½
Medium carrot	½	½
Green pepper	½	½
White vinegar	2 tbsp.	30 mL
Salad dressing (or mayonnaise	1 cup	250 mL
Process cheese spread	½ cup	125 mL

Measure first 5 ingredients into blender. Process until smooth.

Add cheese and purée. Chill. It will thicken when chilled. Makes 2 cups (500 mL).

2 tbsp. (30 mL): 100 Calories; 9 g Total Fat; 224 mg Sodium; 2 g Protein; 3 g Carbohydrate; trace Dietary Fiber

BLUE CHEESE DIP

Add this for variety. Can easily be halved.

Cream cheese, softened	8 oz.	250 g
Blue cheese, crumbled	4 oz.	125 g
Milk	⅔ cup	150 mL
Chopped green onion	¼ cup	60 mL
Worcestershire sauce	1 tsp.	5 mL

Beat all 5 ingredients together in small bowl until smooth. Makes 2⅔ cups (650 mL).

2 tbsp. (30 mL): 63 Calories; 5.6 g Total Fat; 119 mg Sodium; 2 g Protein; 1 g Carbohydrate; trace Dietary Fiber

SPRING DIP

The color of daffodils with orange and green flecks.
Exceptionally good. Best served the same day.

Chopped onion	1 tbsp.	15 mL
Grated carrot, packed	1/3 cup	75 mL
Green pepper, cut up	1/2	1/2
White vinegar	1 tbsp.	15 mL
Salad dressing (or mayonnaise)	1/2 cup	125 mL
Process cheese spread	1/2 cup	125 mL

Place first 4 ingredients in blender. Process until crumbly smooth, not puréed. Place in small bowl.

Add salad dressing and cheese. Stir together well. Makes 2 cups (500 mL).

2 tbsp. (30 mL): 62 Calories; 5.4 g Total Fat; 178 mg Sodium; 1 g Protein; 2 g Carbohydrate; trace Dietary Fiber

CHEESE DIP

Excellent as a vegetable dip. Equally good as a chip dip. Keeps about two weeks in refrigerator.

Envelope dry onion soup mix	1/2 x 1 1/2 oz.	1/2 x 42 g
Process cheese spread	1 cup	250 mL
Sour cream	1 cup	250 mL
Salad dressing (or mayonnaise)	1 cup	250 mL

Measure all 4 ingredients into blender. Process, scraping sides frequently, until thoroughly mixed. Store in refrigerator. Makes 3 cups (750 mL).

2 tbsp. (30 mL): 97 Calories; 8.5 g Total Fat; 315 mg Sodium; 2 g Protein; 3 g Carbohydrate; trace Dietary Fiber

HERB DIP

Vegetables and chips go well with this dip.

Cream cheese, softened	8 oz.	250 g
Plain yogurt	1 cup	250 mL
Salad dressing (or mayonnaise)	1/4 cup	60 mL
Chopped chives	1 tbsp.	15 mL
Ground thyme	1/4 tsp.	1 mL
Garlic powder	1/4 tsp.	1 mL
Salt	1/4 tsp.	1 mL
Celery salt	1/2 tsp.	2 mL
Parsley flakes	1 tsp.	5 mL
Dried sweet basil	1/4 tsp.	1 mL
Onion powder	1/4 tsp.	1 mL
Paprika, for garnish		

Beat all 12 ingredients together in small bowl until smooth. Chill for at least 2 hours before serving. Garnish with paprika. Makes generous 2 cups (500 mL).

2 tbsp. (30 mL): 81 Calories; 7.3 g Total Fat; 160 mg Sodium; 2 g Protein; 2 g Carbohydrate; trace Dietary Fiber

Pictured on page 35.

DOUBLE DILL DIP

Double the pleasure. A treat with veggies.

Sour cream	2 cups	500 mL
Cream cheese, softened	4 oz.	125 g
Parsley flakes	2 tsp.	10 mL
Garlic powder	½ tsp.	2 mL
Onion flakes	2 tsp.	10 mL
Onion salt	1 tsp.	5 mL
Lemon juice	1 tsp.	5 mL
Dill weed	2 tsp.	10 mL
Tangy dill relish	13½ oz.	375 mL

Combine first 8 ingredients in blender. Process until smooth. Turn into medium bowl.

Stir in relish. Makes 4½ cups (1.1 L).

2 tbsp. (30 mL): 33 Calories; 3 g Total Fat; 125 mg Sodium; 1 g Protein; 1 g Carbohydrate; trace Dietary Fiber

AVOCADO DIP

Light and fluffy, this will win your vote.

Cream cheese, softened	8 oz.	250 g
Avocado, peeled and mashed	1	1
Salad dressing (or mayonnaise)	½ cup	125 mL
Lemon juice	1½ tbsp.	25 mL
Garlic powder	⅛ tsp.	0.5 mL
Paprika, sprinkle		

Beat cream cheese, avocado, salad dressing, lemon juice and garlic powder together well in small bowl.

Sprinkle paprika over top. Makes 2½ cups (625 mL).

2 tbsp. (30 mL): 87 Calories; 8.6 g Total Fat; 74 mg Sodium; 1 g Protein; 2 g Carbohydrate; trace Dietary Fiber

dill dips

Enjoy these easy-to-make dips. Dill dips are always good when served with assorted vegetable trays.

★★★★★

Salad dressing (or mayonnaise)	⅔ cup	150 mL
Sour cream	⅔ cup	150 mL
Onion flakes	2 tsp.	10 mL
Parsley flakes	2 tsp.	10 mL
Dill weed	2 tsp.	10 mL
Paprika	¼ tsp.	1 mL
Celery salt	¼ tsp.	1 mL

Mix all 7 ingredients in small bowl. Makes about 1½ cups (375 mL).

2 tbsp. (30 mL): 96 Calories; 9.1 g Total Fat; 128 mg Sodium; 1 g Protein; 3 g Carbohydrate; trace Dietary Fiber

Pictured on page 89.

★★★★★

Light salad dressing (or mayonnaise)	1 cup	250 mL
Low-fat plain yogurt	1 cup	250 mL
Onion powder	¼ tsp.	1 mL
Chopped chives	2 tsp.	10 mL
Dill weed	2 tsp.	10 mL
Celery salt	¼ tsp.	1 mL

Mix all 6 ingredients in small bowl. Chill for at least 1 hour before using. Makes 2 cups (500 mL).

2 tbsp. (30 mL): 54 Calories; 4 g Total Fat; 166 mg Sodium; trace Protein; 4 g Carbohydrate; trace Dietary Fiber

sour cream dips

Only a few ingredients are needed to create these yummy dips.

★★★★★

Sour cream	1 cup	250 mL
Cream cheese, softened	4 oz.	125 g
Imitation bacon bits	2 tsp.	10 mL
Onion flakes, crushed (or chopped chives)	1 tsp.	5 mL

Mix all 4 ingredients in small bowl. Makes 1½ cups (375 mL).

2 tbsp. (30 mL): 67 Calories; 6.3 g Total Fat; 59 mg Sodium; 1 g Protein; 2 g Carbohydrate; trace Dietary Fiber

★★★★★

Light salad dressing (or mayonnaise)	1 cup	250 mL
Low-fat plain yogurt	1 cup	250 mL
Onion powder	¼ tsp.	1 mL
Chopped chives	2 tsp.	10 mL
Dill weed	2 tsp.	10 mL
Celery salt	¼ tsp.	1 mL

Mix all 6 ingredients in small bowl. Chill for at least 1 hour before using. Makes 2 cups (500 mL).

2 tbsp. (30 mL): 54 Calories; 4 g Total Fat; 166 mg Sodium; trace Protein; 4 g Carbohydrate; trace Dietary Fiber

ALL-SEASON DIP

This tangy dip will be a hit! Serve with assorted raw vegetables.

Salad dressing (or mayonnaise)	1 cup	250 mL
Chili sauce	1 cup	250 mL
Onion flakes	3 tbsp.	50 mL
Water	2 tbsp.	30 mL
Mustard seed	2 tsp.	10 mL
Prepared horseradish	2 tbsp.	30 mL

Put all 6 ingredients into small bowl. Stir together well. Chill for at least 2 hours. Makes 2 cups (500 mL).

2 tbsp. (30 mL): 98 Calories; 7.5 g Total Fat; 327 mg Sodium; 1 g Protein; 8 g Carbohydrate; 1 g Dietary Fiber

Use white pepper in creamy dressings to avoid "little black specks." When this is not a concern, use cracked black or mixed peppercorns to produce an appealing look. Chopped fresh dill and parsley also provide a lively contrast to creamy white dressings.

Creamy Dressings

no need to spend money on commercial creamy dressings now that you hold the secret to these great recipes in your hands. After all, nothing beats the fresh flavor of homemade dressings. Whether you choose *Lemon Dressing*, *French Cream Dressing* or *Parmesan Dressing*, you will find a taste to complement any salad.

DOCTORED DRESSING

A very easy make-your-own recipe to have on hand. Use over tossed or with jellied salad.

Salad dressing (or mayonnaise)	2 cups	500 mL
Sour cream	2 cups	500 mL
Granulated sugar	1/4 cup	60 mL
Garlic powder	1/8 tsp.	0.5 mL
Paprika	1/2 tsp.	2 mL
Salt	1/2 tsp.	2 mL
Pepper (white is best)	1/8 tsp.	0.5 mL

Measure all 7 ingredients into medium bowl. Stir together to blend well. Store in covered container in refrigerator. Makes 4 cups (1 L).

2 tbsp. (30 mL): 102 Calories; 9.3 g Total Fat; 140 mg Sodium; 1 g Protein; 4 g Carbohydrate; trace Dietary Fiber

SOUR CREAM DRESSING

A delicious combination.

Sour cream	1 cup	250 mL
Balsamic vinegar	2 tbsp.	30 mL

Mix sour cream and vinegar in small bowl. Makes 1 cup (250 mL).

2 tbsp. (30 mL): 45 Calories; 4.1 g Total Fat; 13 mg Sodium; 1 g Protein; 1 g Carbohydrate; 0 g Dietary Fiber

One way to reduce the fat content when serving salads is simply to use less salad dressing. Dressing should not pool in the bottom of the bowl. Add just enough to coat the salad. With 8 cups (2 L) lightly packed greens, use no more than 1/2 cup (125 mL) creamy dressing, and 1/3 cup (75 mL) when serving an oil and vinegar dressing.

blue cheese dressings

For blue cheese lovers. The strong flavor of blue cheese will jazz up any salad.

★★★★★

Blue cheese, crumbled (use whitest part)	2 tbsp.	30 mL
Salad dressing (or mayonnaise)	½ cup	125 mL
Sour cream	¼ cup	60 mL
White vinegar	1½ tsp.	7 mL
Onion powder	¼ tsp.	1 mL
Garlic powder	¼ tsp.	1 mL

Put all 6 ingredients into blender. Process until smooth. Makes 1 cup (250 mL).

2 tbsp. (30 mL): 93 Calories; 8.9 g Total Fat; 125 mg Sodium; 1 g Protein; 2 g Carbohydrate; trace Dietary Fiber

★★★★★

Salad dressing (or mayonnaise)	1 cup	250 mL
Blue cheese, crumbled	4 oz.	125 g
Onion flakes	1 tsp.	5 mL
Lemon juice	1 tbsp.	15 mL
Granulated sugar	1 tbsp.	15 mL

Mix all 5 ingredients well in small bowl. For a smooth dressing, purée in blender. Chill. Makes 1⅓ cups (325 mL).

2 tbsp. (30 mL): 156 Calories; 14.2 g Total Fat; 297 mg Sodium; 3 g Protein; 5 g Carbohydrate; trace Dietary Fiber

CONDENSED MILK DRESSING

A good choice if you want the taste of vinegar without the strong flavor. Makes a great fruit dip.

Large eggs	2	2
Sweetened condensed milk (see Note)	11 oz.	300 mL
White vinegar	½ cup	125 mL
Dry mustard	1 tsp.	5 mL

Beat eggs together in medium bowl until frothy. Add condensed milk, vinegar and dry mustard. Blend well. Makes 2⅓ cups (575 mL).

2 tbsp. (30 mL): 76 Calories; 2.4 g Total Fat; 33 mg Sodium; 2 g Protein; 12 g Carbohydrate; trace Dietary Fiber

Note: A 14 oz. (398 mL) can may also be used.

CIDER DRESSING: Omit vinegar. Add ¼ cup (60 mL) cider vinegar. Gives a sweeter, different flavor.

The extensive varieties of light, low-fat and non-fat salad dressings and mayonnaises available today offer the solution to cutting back on fat but retaining taste. Try using half salad dressing or mayonnaise and half reduced fat dressing. Flavor may vary only slightly and texture may be a bit softer.

STRAWBERRY DRESSING

Good on fruit salads and jellied salads.

Salad dressing (or mayonnaise)	1 cup	250 mL
Icing (confectioner's) sugar	2 tbsp.	30 mL
Mashed fresh strawberries	¾ cup	175 mL
Envelope dessert topping, prepared according to package directions	½	½

Combine salad dressing, icing sugar and strawberries in medium bowl. Fold in dessert topping. Makes scant 3 cups (750 mL).

2 tbsp. (30 mL): 58 Calories; 5.2 g Total Fat; 63 mg Sodium; trace Protein; 3 g Carbohydrate; trace Dietary Fiber

CREAM CHEESE DRESSING

Yet another yummy cream cheese topping.

Cream cheese, softened	4 oz.	125 g
Icing (confectioner's) sugar	2 tbsp.	30 mL
Cream (or milk)	1 tbsp.	15 mL
Vanilla	½ tsp.	2 mL

Beat all 4 ingredients together well in small bowl. Makes about ½ cup (125 mL).

2 tbsp. (30 mL): 123 Calories; 10.8 g Total Fat; 90 mg Sodium; 2 g Protein; 4 g Carbohydrate; 0 g Dietary Fiber

CRANBERRY DRESSING

A pink dressing to complement your greens.

Cranberry jelly	½ cup	125 mL
Salad dressing (or mayonnaise)	½ cup	125 mL

Whisk both ingredients together in small bowl. Makes 1 cup (250 mL).

2 tbsp. (30 mL): 100 Calories; 7.3 g Total Fat; 98 mg Sodium; trace Protein; 9 g Carbohydrate; trace Dietary Fiber

LEMON DRESSING

A delicious topping. Extra good.

Large egg	1	1
Granulated sugar	¼ cup	60 mL
Lemon juice	¼ cup	60 mL
Envelope dessert topping, prepared according to package directions (see Note)	1	1

Beat egg in medium saucepan with fork. Add sugar and lemon juice. Heat and stir until boiling. Remove from heat. Cool.

Fold dessert topping into cooled lemon mixture. Makes about 2¼ cups (560 mL).

2 tbsp. (30 mL): 29 Calories; 1.2 g Total Fat; 6 mg Sodium; trace Protein; 4 g Carbohydrate; trace Dietary Fiber

Note: 1 cup (250 mL) whipping cream, whipped, can be substituted for the dessert topping.

Creamy dressings have many uses. For a simple salad, tear a mixture of greens into a bowl and toss with any of the dressings in this section. Or, use a creamy dressing the next time you make potato or pasta salad. These dressings can also be spread on bread to jazz up an otherwise ordinary sandwich.

THOUSAND ISLAND DRESSING

Put a ladle in a bowl of this dressing and let guests help themselves. The best!

Salad dressing (or mayonnaise)	2¼ cups	560 mL
Chili sauce	1 cup	250 mL
Sweet pickle relish	½ cup	125 mL
Finely chopped onion	2 tbsp.	30 mL
Hard-boiled eggs	3	3
Chopped pimiento	2 tbsp.	30 mL

Mix salad dressing, chili sauce, pickle relish and onion well in medium bowl.

Chop eggs finely. Add to salad dressing mixture. Add pimiento. Stir together. Store in refrigerator. Makes 4 cups (1 L).

2 tbsp. (30 mL): 103 Calories; 8.7 g Total Fat; 242 mg Sodium; 1 g Protein; 5 g Carbohydrate; 1 g Dietary Fiber

Pictured on page 53 and on back cover.

QUICK THOUSAND ISLAND DRESSING

Nothing could be quicker to mix and serve over your bowl of greens.

Salad dressing (or mayonnaise)	1¼ cups	300 mL
Chili sauce (or ketchup)	½ cup	125 mL
Sweet pickle relish	¼ cup	60 mL
Onion flakes	1 tsp.	5 mL

Combine all 4 ingredients in small bowl. Mix well. Makes 2 cups (500 mL).

2 tbsp. (30 mL): 105 Calories; 9.2 g Total Fat; 248 mg Sodium; trace Protein; 5 g Carbohydrate; 1 g Dietary Fiber

PEANUT SAUCE

This is a perfect dressing for a grilled chicken or spicy chicken salad.

Smooth peanut butter	3 tbsp.	50 mL
Soy sauce	1 tbsp.	15 mL
Cider vinegar	1 tbsp.	15 mL
Water	¼ cup	60 mL
Granulated sugar	1 tsp.	5 mL
Cayenne pepper (or to taste)	⅛ tsp.	0.5 mL

Mix all 6 ingredients in small bowl or shake in jar. Makes scant ⅔ cup (150 mL).

2 tbsp. (30 mL): 11 Calories; 0.8 g Total Fat; 43 mg Sodium; trace Protein; 1 g Carbohydrate; trace Dietary Fiber

PEANUT BUTTER DRESSING

A mellow peanut butter flavor.

Salad dressing (or mayonnaise)	¼ cup	60 mL
Liquid honey	1 tbsp.	15 mL
Smooth peanut butter	1 tbsp.	15 mL

Mix all 3 ingredients well in small bowl. Makes about ⅓ cup (75 mL).

2 tbsp. (30 mL): 169 Calories; 14 g Total Fat; 170 mg Sodium; 2 g Protein; 10 g Carbohydrate; trace Dietary Fiber

PEANUT BUTTER TOPPING: Omit salad dressing. Increase quantity of honey and peanut butter, keeping amounts equal.

TARRAGON DRESSING

This dressing is wonderful over wedges of iceberg lettuce or Chinese cabbage.

Sour cream	½ cup	125 mL
Tarragon vinegar	1 tbsp.	15 mL
Granulated sugar	2 tsp.	10 mL
Onion salt	½ tsp.	2 mL
Paprika	½ tsp.	2 mL

Combine all 5 ingredients in small bowl. Mix well. Makes ½ cup (125 mL).

2 tbsp. (30 mL): 54 Calories; 4.1 g Total Fat; 175 mg Sodium; 1 g Protein; 4 g Carbohydrate; trace Dietary Fiber

CUCUMBER DRESSING

Very flavorful over any kind of greens.

Peeled and diced cucumber	½ cup	125 mL
Sour cream	⅓ cup	75 mL
Lemon juice	1 tsp.	5 mL
Parsley flakes	¼ tsp.	1 mL
Dill weed	¼ tsp.	1 mL
Salt	¼ tsp.	1 mL

Stir all 6 ingredients together in small bowl. Makes ¾ cup (175 mL).

2 tbsp. (30 mL): 21 Calories; 1.8 g Total Fat; 114 mg Sodium; trace Protein; 1 g Carbohydrate; trace Dietary Fiber

Pictured on page 53 and on back cover.

GREEN GODDESS DRESSING

Dressing contains chopped parsley and anchovy paste.

Salad dressing (or mayonnaise)	⅓ cup	75 mL
Sour cream	⅓ cup	75 mL
Chopped green onion	1½ tbsp.	25 mL
Chopped fresh parsley (or ½ tsp., 2 mL, flakes)	1½ tbsp.	25 mL
Anchovy paste	2 tsp.	10 mL
Lemon juice	1½ tsp.	7 mL
Dried tarragon	½ tsp.	2 mL

Combine all 7 ingredients in small bowl. Mix well. Chill for a few hours or overnight. Makes 1 cup (250 mL).

2 tbsp. (30 mL): 68 Calories; 6.4 g Total Fat; 128 mg Sodium; 1 g Protein; 2 g Carbohydrate; trace Dietary Fiber

---

For sensational eye and taste appeal, build a salad using a mix of greens that offer a collage of flavor, texture and color. Some, such as sorrel, which can be rather tart, and endive with its spiky leaves and somewhat buttery taste, should be used sparingly. Glossy watercress, colorful arugula and Belgian endive contribute sharp flavor and contrasting leaf shapes. The familiar Romaine and iceberg offer delicate taste and a satisfying crunch so can be used abundantly. Butter and oakleaf lettuce are soft in texture and lighter in color. Butter lettuce, with its soft and pliable leaves, also forms perfect "cups" or shells for a creamy vegetable or seafood salad. Red leaf lettuce and radicchio add lovely color to complement the greens. A sprinkle of edible flower petals, such as roses, chrysanthemums, violets, dianthus, and others, add the crowning touch to a memorable salad course.

GREEN DRESSING

Has a hint of dill which makes a nice change for a tossed salad.

Salad dressing (or mayonnaise)	½ cup	125 mL
Lemon juice	1 tbsp.	15 mL
Parsley flakes	1 tsp.	5 mL
Dried chives	½ tsp.	2 mL
Dill weed	⅛ tsp.	0.5 mL
Granulated sugar	½ tsp.	2 mL

Mix all 6 ingredients well in small bowl. Let stand before using, preferably overnight. Makes ½ cup (125 mL).

2 tbsp. (30 mL): *150 Calories; 14.6 g Total Fat; 187 mg Sodium; trace Protein; 5 g Carbohydrate; trace Dietary Fiber*

TANGY ORANGE DRESSING

Excellent over a spinach salad.

Low-fat salad dressing (or mayonnaise)	⅔ cup	150 mL
Frozen concentrated orange juice, thawed	⅓ cup	75 mL

Stir salad dressing and orange juice concentrate together in small bowl. Makes 1 cup (250 mL).

2 tbsp. (30 mL): *76 Calories; 5.1 g Total Fat; 154 mg Sodium; trace Protein; 8 g Carbohydrate; trace Dietary Fiber*

Pictured on page 53 and on back cover.

FRENCH CREAM DRESSING

About the tastiest you will find. Super good.

Condensed tomato soup	10 oz.	284 mL
Lemon juice	⅓ cup	75 mL
Liquid honey	⅓ cup	75 mL
White vinegar	3 tbsp.	50 mL
Grated onion	2 tbsp.	30 mL
Worcestershire sauce	2 tsp.	10 mL
Prepared mustard	2 tsp.	10 mL
Salt	1½ tsp.	7 mL
Paprika	1 tsp.	5 mL
Celery seed	½ tsp.	2 mL
Garlic powder	¼ tsp.	1 mL
Cooking oil	¾ cup	175 mL

Measure first 11 ingredients into small bowl. Beat on medium for 3 minutes.

Gradually add cooking oil, beating until all is blended in. Store in refrigerator. Makes 3 cups (750 mL).

2 tbsp. (30 mL): *86 Calories; 7.2 g Total Fat; 258 mg Sodium; trace Protein; 6 g Carbohydrate; trace Dietary Fiber*

To make your own low-fat croutons, take day old bread and cut into cubes. Toss in a mixture of olive oil or cooking oil and your choice of ground or crushed dried herbs. You may also want to add garlic powder or garlic salt. Spread in a single layer on a baking sheet, and bake in 300°F (150°C) oven until crisp and lightly browned. Cool completely. Store in an airtight container in a cool dry place.

COOKED SALAD DRESSING

From a way, way back. This has a lot of zip to it. A little goes a long way.

Granulated sugar	1/2 cup	125 mL
All-purpose flour	2 tbsp.	30 mL
Dry mustard	1 tbsp.	15 mL
Salt	1 tsp.	5 mL
Large eggs	3	3
Milk	1 cup	250 mL
White vinegar	1/2 cup	125 mL
Water	1/2 cup	125 mL

Put sugar, flour, dry mustard and salt in top of double boiler. Stir together until flour is thoroughly mixed in. Beat in eggs, 1 at a time, with spoon.

Stir in milk, vinegar and water. Cook over boiling water, stirring frequently, until thickened. Pour into container. Store covered in refrigerator. Makes about 2 1/2 cups (625 mL).

2 tbsp. (30 mL): 41 Calories; 1 g Total Fat; 146 mg Sodium; 2 g Protein; 7 g Carbohydrate; trace Dietary Fiber

FOR LETTUCE SALADS: Thin dressing with bit of milk or cream. Stir in about 1/2 tsp. (2 mL) granulated sugar or more to taste.

FOR DEVILLED EGGS: Use dressing straight from container. Add salt and pepper to taste according to the number of eggs.

FOR POTATO SALAD: Thin dressing with bit of milk or cream. No extra mustard or vinegar required.

FOR SANDWICHES: Use from container unless milk is needed to moisten sandwich filling. Gives new life to the same tired old sandwiches.

Always keep creamy dressings chilled and stored in an airtight container. If serving on the side, chill the container too. Salads using creamy dressings can be tossed at the last minute or tossed and chilled until ready to serve. Sandwiches made with salad dressings or creamy dressings should never sit for too long at room temperature.

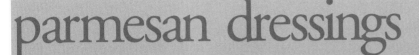

parmesan dressings

These creamy dressings are outstanding over spinach or Romaine lettuce. Very quick to prepare.

★★★★★

Salad dressing (or mayonnaise)	½ cup	125 mL
Grated Parmesan cheese	¼ cup	60 mL
Milk	3 tbsp.	50 mL
Granulated sugar	1 tsp.	5 mL
Dill weed	1 tsp.	5 mL
Lemon pepper	1 tsp.	5 mL
Onion powder	¼ tsp.	1 mL

Shake all 7 ingredients together well in jar. Chill until needed. Shake just before serving. Makes ⅔ cup (150 mL).

2 tbsp. (30 mL): 140 Calories; 12.4 g Total Fat; 233 mg Sodium; 3 g Protein; 5 g Carbohydrate; trace Dietary Fiber

★★★★★

Salad dressing (or mayonnaise)	⅓ cup	75 mL
Grated Parmesan cheese	3 tbsp.	50 mL
Lemon juice	2 tsp.	10 mL
Parsley flakes	½ tsp.	2 mL
Dried sweet basil	¼ tsp.	1 mL
Milk	4 tsp.	20 mL

Combine all 6 ingredients in small bowl. Makes ½ cup (125 mL).

2 tbsp. (30 mL): 130 Calories; 11.6 g Total Fat; 245 mg Sodium; 3 g Protein; 3 g Carbohydrate; trace Dietary Fiber

CURRIED DRESSING

Make it with more or less curry powder. Simply delicious.

Sour cream	¾ cup	175 mL
Lemon juice	1 tsp.	5 mL
Curry powder	½ tsp.	2 mL
Salt	½ tsp.	2 mL

Mix all 4 ingredients in small bowl. Makes ¾ cup (175 mL).

2 tbsp. (30 mL): 45 Calories; 4.1 g Total Fat; 229 mg Sodium; 1 g Protein; 1 g Carbohydrate; trace Dietary Fiber

CAESAR DRESSING

No raw egg or anchovies in this version. Ready in a moment's notice.

Salad dressing (or mayonnaise)	1 cup	250 mL
Lemon juice	1 tbsp.	15 mL
Worcestershire sauce	½ tsp.	2 mL
Garlic powder	¼ tsp.	1 mL
Salt	¼ tsp.	1 mL
Pepper	⅛ tsp.	0.5 mL

Mix all 6 ingredients well in small bowl. Makes 1 cup (250 mL).

2 tbsp. (30 mL): 149 Calories; 14.6 g Total Fat; 271 mg Sodium; trace Protein; 4 g Carbohydrate; trace Dietary Fiber

CREOLE DRESSING

A savory creation. Has a good bite to it.

Hard margarine (or butter)	2 tbsp.	30 mL
Chopped onion	⅔ cup	150 mL
Chopped green pepper	½ cup	125 mL
Canned tomatoes, drained	⅓ cup	75 mL
Granulated sugar	1 tsp.	5 mL
Salt	1 tsp.	5 mL
Pepper	¼ tsp.	1 mL
Hot pepper sauce	¼ tsp.	1 mL
Salad dressing (or mayonnaise)	½ cup	125 mL

Melt margarine in medium frying pan. Add onion and green pepper. Sauté until soft. Cool.

Beat tomatoes, sugar, salt and pepper together in small bowl. Mix in hot pepper sauce and salad dressing. Stir into onion mixture. Makes 2 cups (500 mL).

2 tbsp. (30 mL): 55 Calories; 5.1 g Total Fat; 239 mg Sodium; trace Protein; 2 g Carbohydrate; trace Dietary Fiber

Pictured on page 53 and on back cover.

These bold dressings are bursting with flavor. Serve over a salad tossed with a potpourri of vegetables such as: a mixture of torn greens; grated carrot; finely sliced green, red, white or yellow onion; strips or diced green, red, yellow or orange bell pepper and chopped hard-boiled eggs.

PINK DRESSING

Good over anything.

Salad dressing (or mayonnaise)	1 cup	250 mL
Granulated sugar	¼ cup	60 mL
Walnuts	¼ cup	60 mL
Canned pineapple tidbits, drained	8 oz.	227 mL
Cherry juice	¼ cup	60 mL
Maraschino cherries, chopped	¼ cup	60 mL
Envelope dessert topping, prepared according to package directions (see Note)	¼	¼

Measure first 6 ingredients into blender. Process until smooth. Pour into medium bowl.

Fold dessert topping into pineapple mixture. Makes generous 2 cups (500 mL).

2 tbsp. (30 mL): 111 Calories; 8.8 g Total Fat; 94 mg Sodium; trace Protein; 8 g Carbohydrate; trace Dietary Fiber

Note: ¼ cup (60 mL) whipping cream, whipped, can be substituted for dessert topping.

LIME DRESSING

Tasty over spinach salad.

Salad dressing (or mayonnaise)	¼ cup	60 mL
Lime juice	1 tbsp.	15 mL
Granulated sugar	1 tbsp.	15 mL

Mix salad dressing, lime juice and sugar in small bowl. Stir together. Makes ½ cup (125 mL).

2 tbsp. (30 mL): 125 Calories; 11.1 g Total Fat; 94 mg Sodium; 2 g Protein; 6 g Carbohydrate; 1 g Dietary Fiber

Oil & Vinegar Dressings

freshly made oil dressing can add a subtle or distinctive flavor to any salad. You can add your special touch to any of these dressings. If garlic is your passion, try *Garlic Dressing* or one of the *Caesar Salad Dressings*. Whip up *Oil And Vinegar Dressing* for a classic everyone loves and recognizes.

CHEDDAR CHEESE DRESSING

Excellent to dress spinach salad or any other salad.

Large eggs	2	2
Brown sugar, packed	2 tsp.	10 mL
Salt	1½ tsp.	7 mL
Dry mustard	1 tsp.	5 mL
Worcestershire sauce	1 tsp.	5 mL
Prepared horseradish	1 tsp.	5 mL
Cooking oil	½ cup	125 mL
White vinegar	¼ cup	60 mL
Lemon juice	¼ cup	60 mL
Cooking oil	1½ cups	375 mL
Grated medium Cheddar cheese	1 cup	250 mL
Green onions, finely chopped	3	3

Combine first 6 ingredients in medium bowl. Beat together well.

Gradually add first amount of cooking oil, beating steadily.

Beat vinegar and lemon juice together, alternately with second amount of cooking oil drizzled in. Beat for 2 to 3 minutes. Transfer to blender. Process for about 15 seconds until creamy. Pour into another medium bowl.

Add cheese and green onion. Stir together. Store in refrigerator. Makes about 3½ cups (875 mL).

2 tbsp. (30 mL): 164 Calories; 17.5 g Total Fat; 172 mg Sodium; 2 g Protein; 1 g Carbohydrate; trace Dietary Fiber

OIL AND VINEGAR DRESSING

Such a simple recipe and also one of the most requested. It is better to add oil and vinegar separately to avoid the oil (which stays at the top) all coming out with the very first pouring. Very economical. A lifesaver for lettuce.

White vinegar	3 cups	750 mL
Granulated sugar	4 cups	1 L
Cooking oil, as needed, total approximately	4 cups	1 L

Combine vinegar and sugar in container. Stir, stir and stir! Sugar will eventually dissolve. Store in cool place. Will keep for months. To use, pour equal amounts of oil and vinegar mixture over salad and toss. Cooking oil may be cut down if desired. You will know when you have enough dressing. Too much and it will sink to the bottom of the bowl. Don't sprinkle salt over salad as it takes away the tartness of the dressing. Makes about 4 cups (1 L) vinegar mixture only.

2 tbsp. (30 mL): 172 Calories; 13.8 g Total Fat; trace Sodium; 0 g Protein; 13 g Carbohydrate; 0 g Dietary Fiber

---

Invest in a showy oil and vinegar serving set. This simple way of serving dressing works especially well on a buffet table. But don't just use plain white vinegar. There are many varieties of flavored vinegars available, from the sweeter raspberry to the savory balsamic vinegar. Use a good quality olive oil and you have a low-fat dressing loaded with flavor. If it would be helpful to make your salad ahead of time, place the vinaigrette on the bottom of the bowl, carefully cover with the salad greens, then cover and refrigerate for up to six hours ahead. Toss just before serving.

GARLIC DRESSING

Oil, vinegar and garlic—what a combination!

Cooking oil	½ cup	125 mL
White vinegar	¼ cup	60 mL
Granulated sugar	1 tsp.	5 mL
Garlic powder	½ tsp.	2 mL
Salt	2 tsp.	10 mL
Pepper	½ tsp.	2 mL
Dry mustard	½ tsp.	2 mL

Measure all 7 ingredients into medium bowl. Whisk together. Makes ¾ cup (175 mL).

2 tbsp. (30 mL): 169 Calories; 18.5 g Total Fat; 866 mg Sodium; trace Protein; 2 g Carbohydrate; trace Dietary Fiber

CONTINENTAL DRESSING

Serve this over a vegetable salad.

White vinegar	2 tbsp.	30 mL
Cooking oil	1 tbsp.	15 mL
Water	1 tbsp.	15 mL
Prepared mustard	½ tsp.	2 mL
Salt	½ tsp.	2 mL
Pepper, just a pinch		
Granulated sugar	½-1 tsp.	2-5 mL
Paprika	¼ tsp.	1 mL

Whisk all 8 ingredients together in small bowl. Cover. Chill until ready to serve. Makes ¼ cup (60 mL).

2 tbsp. (30 mL): 65 Calories; 6.7 g Total Fat; 664 mg Sodium; trace Protein; 2 g Carbohydrate; trace Dietary Fiber

SPINACH DRESSING

This is an excellent variation for spinach salad.

Garlic clove, minced	1	1
Cooking oil	6 tbsp.	100 mL
Cider (or red wine) vinegar	2 tbsp.	30 mL
Granulated sugar	1 tsp.	5 mL
Dry mustard	1 tsp.	5 mL
Salt	1 tsp.	5 mL
Pepper	1/2 tsp.	2 mL

Mix all 7 ingredients well in small bowl. Makes 1/2 cup (125 mL).

2 tbsp. (30 mL): 186 Calories; 20.1 g Total Fat; 651 mg Sodium; trace Protein; 2 g Carbohydrate; trace Dietary Fiber

ITALIAN DRESSING

Great for marinating vegetables as well as for greens.

Cooking oil	1 cup	250 mL
Lemon juice	1/4 cup	60 mL
White vinegar	1/4 cup	60 mL
Granulated sugar	2 tsp.	10 mL
Salt	1 tsp.	5 mL
Dry mustard	1/2 tsp.	2 mL
Onion salt	1/2 tsp.	2 mL
Paprika	1/2 tsp.	2 mL
Ground oregano	1/2 tsp.	2 mL
Garlic salt (or 1 clove, crushed)	1/2 tsp.	2 mL
Ground thyme	1/8 tsp.	0.5 mL

Measure all 11 ingredients into jar. Cover. Shake well. Chill for 2 hours before using. Makes 1 1/2 cups (375 mL).

2 tbsp. (30 mL): 169 Calories; 18.5 g Total Fat; 326 mg Sodium; trace Protein; 2 g Carbohydrate; trace Dietary Fiber

Pictured on page 53 and on back cover.

HONEY MUSTARD DRESSING

A tangy dressing. Serve over a combination of vegetables and orange segments.

White vinegar	1/4 cup	60 mL
Prepared mustard	2 tsp.	10 mL
Liquid honey	1/4 cup	60 mL
Cornstarch	2 tsp.	10 mL

Mix all 4 ingredients in small saucepan. Heat and stir until mixture is boiling and thickened. Cool. Makes scant 1/2 cup (125 mL).

2 tbsp. (30 mL): 74 Calories; 0.1 g Total Fat; 37 mg Sodium; trace Protein; 20 g Carbohydrate; trace Dietary Fiber

Pictured on page 53 and on back cover.

FRENCH DRESSING

A regular well-known type of dressing.

White vinegar	1/3 cup	75 mL
Cooking oil	1 cup	250 mL
Granulated sugar	1 tsp.	5 mL
Paprika	1 tsp.	5 mL
Salt	1 tsp.	5 mL
Pepper	1/4 tsp.	1 mL
Cayenne pepper, sprinkle		

Put all 7 ingredients into jar. Cover and shake well. Shake before using. Makes 1 1/3 cups (325 mL).

2 tbsp. (30 mL): 187 Calories; 20.8 g Total Fat; 245 mg Sodium; trace Protein; 1 g Carbohydrate; trace Dietary Fiber

Salad greens should be crisp, clean and quite dry so that the dressing can cling. Greens look more pleasing when torn into bite-size pieces rather than cut. Your guests won't have to fold a piece of lettuce covered with dressing into their mouths when eating. Always be sure to provide a knife and fork when serving salads.

TANGY DRESSING

Drizzle over spinach leaves or mixed greens.

Water	1/3 cup	75 mL
Cornstarch	1 tsp.	5 mL
Granulated sugar	1/3 cup	75 mL
Ketchup	1/3 cup	75 mL
White vinegar	1/4 cup	60 mL
Cooking oil	1 tbsp.	15 mL
Steak sauce	1 tsp.	5 mL
Salt	1 tsp.	5 mL
Pepper	1/8 tsp.	0.5 mL

Stir water and cornstarch together in small saucepan until boiling and thickened.

Stir in sugar until dissolved. Add remaining 6 ingredients. Stir together. Remove from heat. Cool. Makes 1¼ cups (300 mL).

2 tbsp. (30 mL): 49 Calories; 1.4 g Total Fat; 369 mg Sodium; trace Protein; 10 g Carbohydrate; trace Dietary Fiber

RASPBERRY DRESSING

This dressing can be made at least two days in advance. Once it has cooled completely, store in airtight container on shelf.

Whole raspberries (fresh or frozen)	3 cups	750 mL
White vinegar	1 cup	250 mL
Granulated sugar, approximately	1½ cups	375 mL

Place raspberries and vinegar in medium bowl. Stir together. Cover. Let stand on counter for 48 hours. Drain. Measure juice.

Add equal amount of sugar to juice in medium saucepan. Stir often as you bring mixture to a boil. Boil gently for 15 minutes. Cool. Makes 2 cups (500 mL).

2 tbsp. (30 mL): 86 Calories; 0.1 g Total Fat; trace Sodium; trace Protein; 22 g Carbohydrate; 1 g Dietary Fiber

Pictured on page 53 and on back cover.

POPPY SEED DRESSING

Thick and fairly dark. Try it for a change.

Granulated sugar	3/4 cup	175 mL
Dry mustard	1 tsp.	5 mL
Salt	1 tsp.	5 mL
White vinegar	1/3 cup	75 mL
Onion flakes	1 tsp.	5 mL
Cooking oil	1 cup	250 mL
Poppy seed	1½ tbsp.	25 mL
Red food coloring (optional)		

Put sugar, dry mustard, salt, vinegar and onion flakes into blender. Process until smooth.

Add cooking oil in slow steady stream, beating continuously until thickened.

Stir in poppy seed. Add enough coloring to make pleasing pink color. Makes generous 1 cup (250 mL).

2 tbsp. (30 mL): 330 Calories; 28.5 g Total Fat; 326 mg Sodium; trace Protein; 20 g Carbohydrate; trace Dietary Fiber

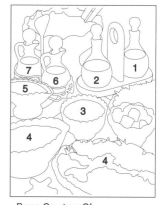

Props Courtesy Of:
Chintz & Company
Eaton's, Stokes

caesar dressings

Several variations of this all-time favorite.
You'll be pleased with any choice!

★★★★★

Garlic clove	1	1
Large egg	1	1
Worcestershire sauce	1 tsp.	5 mL
Lemon juice	2 tbsp.	30 mL
Anchovy paste	2 tsp.	10 mL
Pepper, just a dash		
Cooking oil	1 cup	250 mL

Put first 6 ingredients into blender. Process until smooth. With blender running, add cooking oil in slow stream. Chill for about 2 hours. Makes 1¼ cups (300 mL).

2 tbsp. (30 mL): 207 Calories; 22.7 g Total Fat; 61 mg Sodium; 1 g Protein; trace Carbohydrate; trace Dietary Fiber

★★★★★

Cooking oil	6 tbsp.	100 mL
Red wine vinegar	2 tbsp.	30 mL
Lemon juice	1 tbsp.	15 mL
Egg yolk (large)	1	1
Worcestershire sauce	1 tsp.	5 mL
Garlic powder	¼ tsp.	1 mL
Salt	¼ tsp.	1 mL
Pepper	⅛ tsp.	0.5 mL
Grated Parmesan cheese	½ cup	125 mL

Combine all 9 dressing ingredients in small bowl. Mix well. Makes 1 cup (250 mL).

2 tbsp. (30 mL): 126 Calories; 12.5 g Total Fat; 208 mg Sodium; 3 g Protein; 1 g Carbohydrate; trace Dietary Fiber

Garlic clove, crushed	1	1
Egg yolk (large)	1	1
Lemon juice	1 tbsp.	15 mL
Worcestershire sauce	1 tsp.	5 mL
Cooking (or olive) oil	5 tbsp.	75 mL
Red wine vinegar	2 tbsp.	30 mL
Salt	¼ tsp.	1 mL
Pepper	⅛ tsp.	0.5 mL
Canned anchovies, drained and chopped small	1¾ oz.	50 g
Grated Parmesan cheese	½ cup	125 mL

Combine all 10 ingredients in small bowl. Mix well. Makes 1 cup (250 mL).

2 tbsp. (30 mL): 124 Calories; 11.4 g Total Fat; 428 mg Sodium; 5 g Protein; 1 g Carbohydrate; trace Dietary Fiber

Butter Spreads

hese velvety smooth and creamy old-fashioned butter spreads are delicious smothered on everything from breads to main dishes. Spread strawberry, honey, apple, peach or banana butter on bread, bagels, crackers or muffins. Jazz up meat or seafood with a generous drizzle of melted *Horseradish*, *Parsley* or *Lemon Butter*. These butters are so convenient because you can keep most of them in the refrigerator for several months.

PEACH BUTTER

Good flavored spread for breads of all kinds.

Peeled, pitted and ground peaches (about 3¼ lbs., 1.5 kg), see Note	5 cups	1.25 L
Granulated sugar	1¾ cups	425 mL
Lemon juice	1 tbsp.	15 mL
Almond flavoring	¼ tsp.	1 mL

Combine pulp with sugar, lemon juice and almond flavoring in large saucepan. Bring to a boil, stirring often, for about 1¼ hours or until thickened. A spoonful cooled on chilled saucer should remain smooth with no watery sign. Fill hot sterilized half pint jars to within ¼ inch (6 mm) of top. Place sterilized metal lids on jars and screw metal bands on securely. For added assurance against spoilage, you may choose to process for 5 minutes in a boiling water bath. Makes 2 half pints plus 1 small jar (2¼ cups, 560 mL).

2 tbsp. (30 mL): 102 Calories; 0.1 g Total Fat; trace Sodium; trace Protein; 26 g Carbohydrate; 1 g Dietary Fiber

Pictured on page 71.

Note: Place peaches in boiling water, 2 at a time, for ½ to 1 minute. Peel. Remove pits. Grind or mash peaches.

APRICOT BUTTER: Use apricots instead of peaches. No peeling required.

BANANA BUTTER

A lovely flavored spread for scones, toast or pound cake.

Mashed banana (about 3 medium)	1 cup	250 mL
Canned crushed pineapple, with juice	1 cup	250 mL
Lemon juice	2 tsp.	10 mL
Chopped maraschino cherries	2 tbsp.	30 mL
Granulated sugar	3½ cups	875 mL
Liquid pectin	3 oz.	85 mL

Measure first 5 ingredients into large saucepan. Heat and stir constantly as you bring to a rolling boil. Boil for 1 minute. Remove from heat.

Stir in pectin. Stir and skim for 5 minutes so fruit won't float. Pour into hot sterilized half pint jars to within ¼ inch (6 mm) of top. Place sterilized metal lids on jars and screw metal bands on securely. For added assurance against spoilage, you may choose to process for 5 minutes in a boiling water bath. Makes 4 half pints (4 cups, 1 L).

2 tbsp. (30 mL): 97 Calories; trace Total Fat; trace Sodium; trace Protein; 25 g Carbohydrate; trace Dietary Fiber

Whip, then pipe any of the fruit butters into rosettes, or swirl in a pretty bowl. Another idea is to cut into shapes relating to your party theme, i.e. balloons for a birthday, stars for Christmas, miniature footballs for a sports gathering, etc. It's surprisingly easy—chill flavored butter until you can roll it on a sheet of waxed paper placed on a baking sheet. Re-chill until firm and cut into shapes with cookie cutters. Or, roll softened butter into a log shape. Chill and then slice into rounds.

strawberry butters

Try these small recipes first. Serve with muffins, biscuits or loaves. Delicious.

★★★★★

Fresh whole strawberries	3 cups	750 mL
Lemon juice	2 tbsp.	30 mL
Granulated sugar	2 cups	500 mL

Grind or mash strawberries. Measure 2 cups (500 mL) and combine with remaining 2 ingredients in medium saucepan. Heat and stir until sugar is dissolved. Bring to a boil. Boil for about 35 minutes. A spoonful cooled on chilled saucer should remain smooth with no watery sign. Fill hot sterilized half pint jar to within ¼ inch (6 mm) of top. Place sterilized metal lid on sealer and screw metal band on securely. For added assurance against spoilage, you may choose to process for 5 minutes in a boiling water bath. Makes 1 half pint plus 1 small jar (1¼ cups, 300 mL).

2 tbsp. (30 mL): 168 Calories; 0.2 g Total Fat; 1 mg Sodium; trace Protein; 43 g Carbohydrate; 1 g Dietary Fiber

★★★★★

Butter (or hard margarine), softened	½ cup	125 mL
Strawberry jam	½ cup	125 mL
Fresh strawberries, mashed	½ cup	125 mL

Beat butter in medium bowl until fluffy. Add jam and beat together well. Mix in strawberries. Makes 1½ cups (375 mL).

2 tbsp. (30 mL): 109 Calories; 7.9 g Total Fat; 93 mg Sodium; trace Protein; 10 g Carbohydrate; trace Dietary Fiber

PLUM BUTTER

This can be thickened in the oven or on top of the stove. A dark butter. A delicious spread.

Fresh prune plums, halved and pitted	2½ lbs.	1.1 kg
Granulated sugar	2¼ cups	560 mL
Lemon juice	1 tbsp.	15 mL
Ground cinnamon	¼ tsp.	1 mL

Grind plums or run through food processor. Turn into ungreased 9 x 13 inch (22 x 33 cm) pan.

Add remaining 3 ingredients. Stir. Cook in 325°F (160°C) oven, stirring every 30 minutes until thickened. This will take about 2½ hours. Pulp may also be cooked in large saucepan, stirring occasionally at first, then more often as it thickens. A spoonful cooled on chilled saucer should remain smooth with no watery sign. Pour into hot sterilized half pint jars to within ¼ inch (6 mm) of top. Place sterilized metal lids on jars and screw metal bands on securely. For added assurance against spoilage, you may choose to process for 5 minutes in a boiling water bath. Makes 2 half pints plus 1 small jar (2¼ cups, 560 mL).

2 tbsp. (30 mL): 129 Calories; 0.4 g Total Fat; trace Sodium; trace Protein; 33 g Carbohydrate; 1 g Dietary Fiber

To store flavored butters (made with butter or hard margarine), wrap well in plastic and place in airtight container in the refrigerator. Try to use up quickly as the added fruit or herbs will soon lose their flavor and texture. Butters made with fruit and pectin should be processed in a water bath and stored in a cool, dry, dark place.

PARSLEY BUTTER

Put a dab on each plate beside or over fish.

Butter (or hard margarine)	¼ cup	60 mL
Chopped fresh parsley	2 tbsp.	30 mL
Chopped chives	1 tsp.	5 mL
Onion salt	⅛ tsp.	0.5 mL

Mix all 4 ingredients well in small bowl. Chill for 2 to 3 hours so flavors can mingle. Makes ¼ cup (60 mL).

2 tbsp. (30 mL): 211 Calories; 23.5 g Total Fat; 354 mg Sodium; trace Protein; 1 g Carbohydrate; trace Dietary Fiber

Pictured on front cover.

WHITE BUTTER

Exceptionally good served on broiled fish.

Chopped chives	2 tsp.	10 mL
White vinegar	½ cup	125 mL
Butter (or hard margarine)	½ cup	125 mL
Salt	½ tsp.	2 mL
Pepper	⅛ tsp.	0.5 mL

Put chives and vinegar into small saucepan. Bring to a boil. Simmer until almost all vinegar is evaporated. Remove from heat. Cool. Set pan in cold water to hasten cooling.

Mix in butter, bit by bit, then add salt and pepper. Mix well. Makes ½ cup (125 mL).

2 tbsp. (30 mL): 213 Calories; 23.5 g Total Fat; 601 mg Sodium; trace Protein; 2 g Carbohydrate; trace Dietary Fiber

MAÎTRE D'HÔTEL BUTTER

Try this well-known butter on meat steaks or fish steaks.

Butter (or hard margarine), softened	½ **cup**	125 mL
Finely chopped fresh parsley (or ¾ tsp., 4 mL, flakes)	1 **tbsp.**	15 mL
Lemon juice	1 **tbsp.**	15 mL
Pepper	⅛ **tsp.**	0.5 mL

Cream butter and parsley together in small bowl. Add lemon juice, a few drops at a time, creaming after each addition. Mix in pepper. Chill until almost firm. Shape into small log. Roll in waxed paper. Keep chilled. When firm, cut into slices to serve. Makes ½ cup (125 mL).

2 tbsp. (30 mL): 211 Calories; 23.5 g Total Fat; 275 mg Sodium; trace Protein; 1 g Carbohydrate; trace Dietary Fiber

Variation: Add about 2 tsp. (10 mL) chopped chives to margarine before rolling into log.

HORSERADISH BUTTER

Put a coin of this onto meat or fish as you serve it. Tangy and good.

Butter (or hard margarine), softened	½ **cup**	125 mL
Prepared horseradish	1 **tbsp.**	15 mL
Worcestershire sauce	1 **tsp.**	5 mL

Cream all 3 ingredients together in small bowl. Chill until almost firm. Shape into log. Roll in waxed paper. Chill until hard. Slice into coins to serve. Makes ½ cup (125 mL).

2 tbsp. (30 mL): 212 Calories; 23.5 g Total Fat; 293 mg Sodium; trace Protein; 1 g Carbohydrate; trace Dietary Fiber

HONEY BUTTER

Super easy. A smooth texture for easy spreading on tea loaves, muffins, pancakes and waffles.

Butter (or hard margarine), softened	½ **cup**	125 mL
Liquid honey	¼ **cup**	60 mL

Beat butter and honey together in small bowl until mixed. Makes ¾ cup (175 mL).

2 tbsp. (30 mL): 181 Calories; 15.6 g Total Fat; 159 mg Sodium; trace Protein; 12 g Carbohydrate; trace Dietary Fiber

LEMON BUTTER

Smother your vegetables in this.

Butter (or hard margarine)	½ cup	125 mL
Lemon juice	2 tbsp.	30 mL
Worcestershire sauce	½ tsp.	2 mL

Melt all 3 ingredients together in small saucepan. Makes ½ cup (125 mL).

2 tbsp. (30 mL): 212 Calories; 23.5 g Total Fat; 281 mg Sodium; trace Protein; 1 g Carbohydrate; trace Dietary Fiber

APPLE BUTTER

One of the most used spreads. Great on muffins and loaves. Also good on a pork sandwich.

Tart apples	4 lbs.	1.8 kg
Granulated sugar	2 cups	500 mL
Lemon juice	3 tbsp.	50 mL
Ground cinnamon	1 tsp.	5 mL

Remove stems and blossom ends from apples. Cut into quarters. Place in large stock pot, including seeds, cores and peel. Add sugar, lemon juice and cinnamon. Stir together. Let stand until apples release some juice. Cover. Heat slowly. Bring to a boil. Cook gently, stirring often, until apples are tender. Press through food mill. Turn pulp into small enamel roaster. Bake, uncovered, in 325°F (160°C) oven for 2 to 2½ hours, stirring every 30 minutes until thickened. A spoonful cooled on chilled saucer should remain smooth with no watery sign. This may also be cooked in large stock pot on top of stove, stirring often. Pour into hot sterilized half pint jars to within ¼ inch (6 mm) of top. Place sterilized metal lids on jars and screw metal bands on securely. For added assurance against spoilage, you may choose to process for 5 minutes in a boiling water bath. Makes 4 half pints (4 cups, 1 L).

2 tbsp. (30 mL): 79 Calories; 0.2 g Total Fat; trace Sodium; trace Protein; 20 g Carbohydrate; 1 g Dietary Fiber

Flavored butters are a lovely treat at the breakfast table with warm muffins or toast. Or, try a fruit butter with tea loaves or scones. The herbed butters perk up fish, seafood, beef or poultry dishes and can replace butter or margarine to liven up those lunchbox or party sandwiches.

Cheese Balls

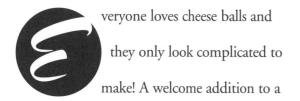

Everyone loves cheese balls and they only look complicated to make! A welcome addition to a cheese tray or as an irresistible appetizer on the buffet table, these tempting recipes may be made ahead of time and refrigerated until needed. Curry lovers will adore the *Round Cheese Ball* and blue cheese fans aren't forgotten with a piquant ball featuring three cheeses, including their favorite.

ROUND CHEESE SPREAD

Nice strong curry flavor.

Cream cheese, softened	8 oz.	250 g
Salad dressing (or mayonnaise)	1 tbsp.	15 mL
Curry powder	1½ tsp.	7 mL
Worcestershire sauce	1 tsp.	5 mL
Seasoning salt	¼ tsp.	1 mL
Salt	¼ tsp.	1 mL
Paprika	¼ tsp.	1 mL
Chutney, your choice	½ cup	125 mL

Beat first 7 ingredients together on medium. Shape into flattened ball. Chill.

When ready to use, place cheese round on serving plate. Spoon chutney over top allowing some to run down sides, using more chutney if desired. Makes 1½ cups (375 mL).

2 tbsp. (30 mL): 88 Calories; 7.6 g Total Fat; 154 mg Sodium; 2 g Protein; 4 g Carbohydrate; trace Dietary Fiber

DATE NUT LOG

Serve with assorted crackers.

Cream cheese, softened	8 oz.	250 g
Corn syrup	2 tbsp.	30 mL
Maple flavoring	½ tsp.	2 mL
Chopped dates	¾ cup	175 mL
Chopped walnuts	½ cup	125 mL
Finely chopped walnuts	¾ cup	175 mL

Beat cream cheese, corn syrup and maple flavoring together in small bowl until smooth.

Stir in dates and first amount of walnuts. Chill overnight. Shape into log.

Roll in remaining walnuts. Chill until ready to serve. May be frozen. Makes 3 cups (750 mL).

2 tbsp. (30 mL): 95 Calories; 7.6 g Total Fat; 32 mg Sodium; 2 g Protein; 6 g Carbohydrate; 1 g Dietary Fiber

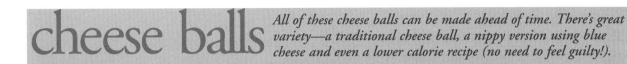

★★★★★★★★★★★★★★★★★★★★★★★★★★★★★★★★★

Dips, Spreads & Dressings

cheese balls

All of these cheese balls can be made ahead of time. There's great variety—a traditional cheese ball, a nippy version using blue cheese and even a lower calorie recipe (no need to feel guilty!).

★★★★★

Cream cheese, softened	2 x 8 oz.	2 x 250 g
Grated sharp Cheddar cheese	2 cups	500 mL
Finely chopped pimiento	1 tbsp.	15 mL
Finely chopped green pepper	1 tbsp.	15 mL
Finely chopped onion	1 tbsp.	15 mL
Worcestershire sauce	2 tsp.	10 mL
Lemon juice	1 tsp.	5 mL
Salt	1/8 tsp.	0.5 mL
Cayenne pepper	1/8 tsp.	0.5 mL
Chopped walnuts (or pecans or parsley)	1/2 cup	125 mL

Mix first 9 ingredients well. Shape into 1 or more balls or logs.

Roll in walnuts. Makes 4 cups (1 L).

2 tbsp. (30 mL): 94 Calories; 8.8 g Total Fat; 103 mg Sodium; 3 g Protein; 1 g Carbohydrate; trace Dietary Fiber

★★★★★

Cream cheese, softened	8 oz.	250 g
Blue cheese, softened	4 oz.	125 g
Grated medium Cheddar cheese	2 cups	500 mL
Chopped pecans (or walnuts)	1/2 cup	125 mL
Parsley flakes	1 tbsp.	15 mL
Worcestershire sauce	1 tsp.	5 mL
Onion powder	1/2 tsp.	2 mL
Chopped pecans (or walnuts)	1/2 cup	125 mL

Combine first 7 ingredients in large bowl. Mix thoroughly. Shape into ball.

Put second amount of pecans onto working surface. Roll cheese ball to coat. Chill. Bring to room temperature before serving for best flavor. Makes 4 cups (1 L).

2 tbsp. (30 mL): 93 Calories; 8.6 g Total Fat; 121 mg Sodium; 3 g Protein; 1 g Carbohydrate; trace Dietary Fiber

Low-fat cottage cheese, rinsed and well drained	2 cups	500 mL
Hard margarine (or butter), softened	1/2 cup	125 mL
Grated low-fat sharp Cheddar cheese	2 cups	500 mL
Chopped pimiento	1 tbsp.	15 mL
Chopped green pepper	1 tbsp.	15 mL
Onion flakes	1 1/2 tbsp.	25 mL
Worcestershire sauce	1 tbsp.	15 mL
Lemon juice	2 tsp.	10 mL
Cayenne pepper	1/8 tsp.	0.5 mL
Chopped fresh parsley	1/2 cup	125 mL

Place cottage cheese and margarine in blender or food processor. Process until smooth.

Combine next 7 ingredients in large bowl. Add blender contents. Mix well. Chill for several hours or overnight.

Shape into ball. Roll in parsley. Chill. Makes 3 1/2 cups (875 mL).

2 tbsp. (30 mL): 65 Calories; 5 g Total Fat; 244 mg Sodium; 4 g Protein; 2 g Carbohydrate; trace Dietary Fiber

STUFFED EDAM

Serve at room temperature. Can be made the day before and stored in the refrigerator. Very tasty.

Edam cheese, with red wax coating (or Gouda)	1 lb.	454 g
Cream cheese, softened	8 oz.	250 g
Apricot jam	¼ cup	60 mL
Onion powder	½ tsp.	2 mL
Paprika	⅛ tsp.	0.5 mL
Milk	1-2 tbsp.	15-30 mL
Finely chopped red pepper	⅓ cup	75 mL
Chopped chives	1 tsp.	5 mL

Cut a thin slice from top of cheese. Use sharp knife to cut zigzag edge if you like. Use spoon or melon baller to scoop out cheese, leaving shell intact. Dice cheese into small pieces.

Beat cream cheese, jam, onion powder and paprika together in small bowl. Add Edam cheese. Stir together. Process in food processor for 1 minute. Add milk. Process for 20 seconds. Remove to bowl.

Add green pepper and chives. Stir together. Spoon into red shell. Makes 2½ cups (625 mL).

2 tbsp. (30 mL): 132 Calories; 10.3 g Total Fat; 247 mg Sodium; 6 g Protein; 4 g Carbohydrate; trace Dietary Fiber

BAKED CHEESE

A round of nutty coated cheese that is just yummy.

Brie (or Camembert) cheese round	1 x 4½ oz.	1 x 125 g
Hard margarine (or butter), softened	2 tbsp.	30 mL
Brown sugar, packed	2 tbsp.	30 mL
Sliced hazelnuts	¼ cup	60 mL

Place cheese in ungreased 9 inch (22 cm) pie plate.

Cream margarine and brown sugar together in medium bowl. Spread over top and sides of cheese.

Sprinkle hazelnuts over top. Press lightly into cheese. Bake, uncovered, in 350°F (175°C) oven for 15 to 20 minutes to heat through. Makes 1 cup (250 mL).

2 tbsp. (30 mL): 157 Calories; 13.1 g Total Fat; 110 mg Sodium; 6 g Protein; 2 g Carbohydrate; trace Dietary Fiber

Lend some pizzazz to bland-looking cheese balls by surrounding them with color. Sprigs of fresh parsley or coriander, or slim fingers of carrots, zucchini, red and green peppers and celery, will liven up the platter. Don't forget to include a brightly-colored cheese spreader.

CHEESE ROLL

You may want to double this exceptionally tasty treat.

Cream cheese, softened	4 oz.	125 g
Grated medium or sharp Cheddar cheese	1½ cups	375 mL
Process cheese spread, softened	⅓ cup	75 mL
Onion powder	¼ tsp.	1 mL
Cayenne pepper	⅛ tsp.	0.5 mL
Finely chopped pecans	⅓ cup	75 mL

Mix first 5 ingredients well. Chill for 45 minutes. Shape into roll about 8 inches (20 cm) long.

Roll in pecans, covering completely. Wrap and chill. Remove from refrigerator 20 to 30 minutes before serving. Makes 1 roll or about 32 rounds.

1 round without cracker: 53 Calories; 4.7 g Total Fat; 91 mg Sodium; 2 g Protein; 1 g Carbohydrate; trace Dietary Fiber

Pictured on page 35.

LAST MINUTE APPETIZER

Horseradish gives an unexpected tang.

Apple (or crabapple) jelly	½ cup	125 mL
Pineapple (or apricot) jam	½ cup	125 mL
Prepared horseradish	1 tbsp.	15 mL
Dry mustard, generous measure	¼ tsp.	1 mL
Cream cheese, softened	8 oz.	250 g

Put first 4 ingredients into small bowl. Stir together well.

Place cream cheese on serving dish. Top with jam mixture, allowing it to run down sides. Serve with assorted crackers. Makes 1 cup (250 mL) sauce plus 1 block cream cheese.

1 tbsp. (15 mL) sauce plus 1 tbsp. (15 mL) cream cheese: 106 Calories; 5.3 g Total Fat; 48 mg Sodium; 1 g Protein; 14 g Carbohydrate; trace Dietary Fiber

Serve cheese balls with an assortment of hard crackers, as soft fragile crackers will break too easily with the pressure of spreading. Cheese balls containing nippy blue cheese are also a perfect complement to a fruit tray.

Nutty Cheese Ball

Serve with assorted fruit and crackers. Somewhat softer ball. Make the day before.

Canned crushed pineapple, well drained	14 oz.	398 mL
Cream cheese, softened	12 oz.	375 g
Salt	1 tsp.	5 mL
Onion powder	¼ tsp.	1 mL
Chopped pecans	¾ cup	175 mL
Chopped green pepper	2 tbsp.	30 mL

Combine pineapple, cream cheese, salt and onion powder in medium bowl. Beat together slowly.

Mix in pecans and green pepper. Chill overnight. Shape into ball. Serve with fruit and assorted crackers. Makes 3 cups (750 mL).

2 tbsp. (30 mL): 78 Calories; 7.3 g Total Fat; 153 mg Sodium; 1 g Protein; 2 g Carbohydrate; trace Dietary Fiber

Nutty Crab Ball

Cream cheese is the base for this instead of Cheddar. It has an orange color and good flavor with a bit of a bite. May be made ahead of time wrapped snugly in two layers of plastic wrap, then in foil, and frozen.

Cream cheese, softened	8 oz.	250 g
Ketchup	1 tbsp.	15 mL
Lemon juice	2 tsp.	10 mL
Pimiento-stuffed olives, finely chopped	6	6
Worcestershire sauce	½ tsp.	2 mL
Onion powder	1 tsp.	5 mL
Canned crabmeat, drained and cartilage removed, flaked	4.2 oz.	120 g
Chopped pecans	½ cup	125 mL

Beat or mash first 7 ingredients together in medium bowl. Chill for about 1 hour until it is firm enough to shape into ball.

Roll in pecans. Chill. Best served at room temperature. Makes 2¼ cups (560 mL).

2 tbsp. (30 mL): 76 Calories; 7.1 g Total Fat; 119 mg Sodium; 2 g Protein; 1 g Carbohydrate; trace Dietary Fiber

To crush walnuts or other nuts easily and to keep them from spilling all over the floor, place them in a larger plastic freezer bag. Do not close or seal the bag and make sure it is considerably larger than the quantity of nuts you are using. Take a rolling pin and gently pound and roll until the nuts are the consistency that you need.

Jams

Transforming a harvest of luscious fruit and vegetables into bright jars of preserves remains a time-honored ritual for many. But time is precious for everyone and these simple recipes will reduce your time in the kitchen. Freezer jams have been welcomed in recent years as a speedier but still-delicious alternative.

PEACH CONSERVE

Little cherry pieces are very colorful in this good conserve. A bit softer than marmalade. Also called Peach Jam.

Peaches, peeled and cut into small pieces, reserve pits	12	12
Orange, thinly peeled, white pith removed and discarded, reserve peel	1	1
Lemon with peel, cut up and seeded	1	1
Salt	¼ tsp.	1 mL
Granulated sugar, approximately	4 cups	1 L
Jar maraschino cherries, drained and halved or quartered	8 oz.	250 mL

Place peaches, 2 at a time, in boiling water for ½ to 1 minute. Peel. Put peaches and pits into large stock pot. Grind orange peel, orange pulp and lemon. Add to pot.

Stir in salt. Measure bulk of fruit and add same amount of sugar. Proportion is 1 cup (250 mL) fruit mixture to 1 cup (250 mL) sugar. Boil for about 1 hour, stirring occasionally. Discard pits. Mixture will be soft but not too runny.

Add cherries just before filling jars. Fill hot sterilized half pint jars to within ¼ inch (6 mm) of top. Place sterilized metal lids on jars and screw metal bands on securely. For added assurance against spoilage, you may choose to process in a boiling water bath for 5 minutes. Makes 8 half pints (8 cups, 2 L).

2 tbsp. (30 mL): 58 Calories; trace Total Fat; 10 mg Sodium; trace Protein; 15 g Carbohydrate; 1 g Dietary Fiber

Pictured on page 71.

ZUCCHINI PEACH JAM

A superb taste for a bargain jam.

Peeled and grated zucchini (5-6 medium)	6 cups	1.5 L
Granulated sugar	6 cups	1.5 L
Canned crushed pineapple, with juice	¾ cup	175 mL
Lemon juice	½ cup	125 mL
Peach-flavored gelatin (jelly powder)	2 × 3 oz.	2 × 85 g

Stir zucchini and sugar together in large stock pot. Heat, stirring occasionally, until mixture comes to a boil. Boil gently for 15 minutes, stirring occasionally.

Add pineapple with juice and lemon juice. Stir together. Return to a boil. Boil for 6 minutes, stirring occasionally.

Stir in gelatin until it is dissolved. Skim off foam. Pour into hot sterilized half pint jars to within ¼ inch (6 mm) of top. Place sterilized metal lids on jars and screw metal bands on securely. For added assurance against spoilage, you may choose to process in a boiling water bath for 5 minutes. Makes 8 half pints (8 cups, 2 L).

2 tbsp. (30 mL): 87 Calories; trace Total Fat; 8 mg Sodium; 1 g Protein; 22 g Carbohydrate; trace Dietary Fiber

GOOSEBERRY JAM

Just the right tartness.

Granulated sugar	4 cups	1 L
Water	2 cups	500 mL
Gooseberries, tipped and stemmed, about 4 cups (1 L)	2 lbs.	900 g

Combine sugar and water in large pot. Heat and stir together until sugar is dissolved. Bring to a boil. Boil for 15 minutes, stirring occasionally.

Add gooseberries. Return to a boil. Boil for about 30 minutes. Skim off foam. Cool teaspoonful on chilled saucer to see if it jells. If mixture doesn't jell, return to heat for 2 minutes and test again. Repeat until jelly stage has been reached. Pour into hot sterilized half pint jars to within ¼ inch (6 mm) of top. Place sterilized metal lids on jars and screw metal bands on securely. For added assurance against spoilage, you may choose to process in a boiling water bath for 5 minutes. Makes 4 half pints (4 cups, 1 L).

2 tbsp. (30 mL): 109 Calories; 0.2 g Total Fat; 1 mg Sodium; trace Protein; 28 g Carbohydrate; 1 g Dietary Fiber

The gel point for jam is 221 to 224°F (105 to 107°C); for jelly it's 220°F (104°C). Use a candy thermometer for most accurate results.

SAVORY TOMATO JAM

Delicious spread on meat as well as toast.

Ripe tomatoes	5 lbs.	2.3 kg
Grated peel of 1 lemon	4 tsp.	20 mL
Lemon juice	½ cup	125 mL
Granulated sugar	4 cups	1 L
White vinegar	2 cups	500 mL
Ground cinnamon	2 tsp.	10 mL
Coarse (pickling) salt	1 tsp.	5 mL

Place tomatoes in boiling water for about 1 minute until the skins crack slightly. Peel, remove stem ends and cores and cut up. Place in large stock pot. Slowly bring to a boil, stirring occasionally. Boil for 20 to 30 minutes, stirring occasionally, until liquid is reduced.

Add lemon peel, lemon juice, sugar, vinegar, cinnamon and salt. Stir as mixture returns to a boil. Boil for about 40 minutes, stirring often, until thickened. Skim off foam. Cool teaspoonful on chilled saucer to see if it jells. If mixture doesn't jell, return to heat for 2 minutes and test again. Repeat until jelly stage has been reached. Fill hot sterilized half pint jars to within ¼ inch (6 mm) of top. Place sterilized metal lids on jars and screw metal bands on securely. For added assurance against spoilage, you may choose to process in a boiling water bath for 5 minutes. Makes 4 half pints (4 cups,1 L).

2 tbsp. (30 mL): 113 Calories; 0.2 g Total Fat; 87 mg Sodium; 1 g Protein; 29 g Carbohydrate; 1 g Dietary Fiber

STRAWBERRY JAM

Everyone's favorite spread.

Whole fresh strawberries, hulled and cut up	4 lbs.	1.8 kg
Granulated sugar	10 cups	2.5 L
Frozen concentrated apple juice	¼ cup	60 mL
Lemon juice	2 tbsp.	30 mL

Combine strawberries, sugar, concentrated apple juice and lemon juice in large pot. Stir until sugar is dissolved and mixture comes to a full rolling boil. Boil rapidly for about 20 minutes. Skim off foam. Cool teaspoonful on chilled saucer to see if it jells. If mixture doesn't jell, return to heat for 2 minutes and test again. Repeat until jelly stage has been reached. Fill hot sterilized pint jars to within ½ inch (12 mm) of top. Place sterilized metal lids on jars and screw metal bands on securely. For added assurance against spoilage, you may choose to process in a boiling water bath for 5 minutes. Makes 5 pints (5 cups,1.25 L).

2 tbsp. (30 mL): 209 Calories; 0.2 g Total Fat; 1 mg Sodium; trace Protein; 54 g Carbohydrate; 1 g Dietary Fiber

---

Drop a teaspoonful of jelly or jam on a well-chilled saucer. For convenience, put several saucers into the freezer at the start of the process. The jelly or jam should "set" in about two minutes. Test for setting by holding the saucer on its side; the jelly or jam should move very slowly. Another test is to run the spoon tip through the center; the "path" should remain open. If not set, continue boiling in two-minute intervals and retest.

STRAWBERRY FREEZER JAM

This has the best color and the freshest flavor of all jams.

Whole fresh strawberries, hulled	5 cups	1.25 L
Granulated sugar	4 cups	1 L
Lemon juice	2 tbsp.	30 mL
Liquid pectin	3 oz.	85 mL

Mash strawberries to make about 1¾ cups (425 mL). Combine with sugar in large bowl. Let stand for 10 minutes.

Add lemon juice and pectin to fruit mixture. Stir continually for 3 minutes. Fill freezer containers leaving at least 1 inch (2.5 cm) head space for expansion when frozen. Cover with tight fitting lid. Let stand on counter for up to 24 hours until set. Freeze. Refrigerate once opened. Makes 5 half pints (5 cups, 1.25 L).

2 tbsp. (30 mL): 83 Calories; 0.1 g Total Fat; trace Sodium; trace Protein; 21 g Carbohydrate; trace Dietary Fiber

RASPBERRY FREEZER JAM: Use 2 cups (500 mL) mashed raspberries instead of strawberries.

COOKED STRAWBERRY FREEZER JAM

Excellent flavor and color. Soft enough to serve over ice cream.

Sliced fresh strawberries, hulled	4 cups	1 L
Granulated sugar	2 cups	500 mL
Granulated sugar	2 cups	500 mL
Lemon juice	2 tbsp.	30 mL

Place strawberries in large stock pot. Cover with first amount of sugar. Heat and stir until mixture comes to a full rolling boil. Boil hard for 3 minutes, stirring continually.

Add second amount of sugar. Return to a boil, stirring continually. Boil hard for 3 minutes, stirring continually. Remove from heat.

Add lemon juice. Stir. Skim off foam. Cool. Fill freezer containers leaving at least 1 inch (2.5 cm) head space for expansion when frozen. Cover with tight fitting lid. Let stand on counter for 24 hours to set. Freeze. Makes 4 half pints (4 cups, 1 L).

2 tbsp. (30 mL): 103 Calories; 0.1 g Total Fat; trace Sodium; trace Protein; 26 g Carbohydrate; trace Dietary Fiber

Choose fruit that is just ripe and not bruised. Overripe fruit will mush easier and contains less natural pectin. Bruising may cause spoilage to occur regardless of how careful you might be with the canning process; it will also spoil the taste.

PEACH FREEZER JAM

A fresh peach taste for the middle of winter.

Peeled, pitted and mashed peaches, about 1 lb. (454 g)	1 cup	250 mL
Granulated sugar	2¾ cups	675 mL
Light corn syrup	½ cup	125 mL
Lemon juice	1 tbsp.	15 mL
Liquid pectin	3 oz.	85 mL

Combine peach, sugar, syrup and lemon juice in medium bowl. Stir together well. Let stand for 10 minutes.

Add pectin. Stir until sugar is dissolved. Fill freezer containers leaving at least 1 inch (2.5 cm) head space for expansion when frozen. Cover with tight fitting lid. Freeze. Refrigerate for up to 1 month once opened. Makes 3½ cups (875 mL).

2 tbsp. (30 mL): 99 Calories; trace Total Fat; 4 mg Sodium; trace Protein; 26 g Carbohydrate; trace Dietary Fiber

PEACH STRAWBERRY JAM: Use half mashed peaches and half mashed strawberries.

RASPBERRY JAM

Real raspberry jam. Dark red in color.

Fresh raspberries, packed	4 cups	1 L
Granulated sugar	3 cups	750 mL
Lemon juice	1 tbsp.	15 mL

Place raspberries in large stock pot. Cover with sugar. Stir together. Let stand on counter for 1 to 2 hours until berries release their juice.

Add lemon juice. Heat, stirring occasionally, until mixture begins to bubble. Simmer slowly, stirring until sugar is dissolved. Increase heat to high and bring to a rolling boil. Boil hard for about 20 minutes, stirring occasionally, until mixture thickens. Skim off foam. Cool teaspoonful on chilled saucer to see if it jells. If mixture doesn't jell, return to heat for 2 minutes and test again. Repeat until jelly stage has been reached. Fill hot sterilized half pint jars to within ¼ inch (6 mm) of top. Place sterilized metal lids on jars and screw metal bands on securely. For added assurance against spoilage, you may choose to process in a boiling water bath for 5 minutes. Makes 2 half pints plus 1 small jar (2¼ cups, 560 mL).

2 tbsp. (30 mL): 143 Calories; 0.2 g Total Fat; trace Sodium; trace Protein; 37 g Carbohydrate; 1 g Dietary Fiber

LOGANBERRY JAM: Use loganberries instead of raspberries.

BLACKBERRY JAM: Use blackberries instead of raspberries.

Pretty jars of colorful jam, jellies or marmalades are always a much-appreciated gift. Don't forget to attach a fancy name label and a tie of raffia or ribbon. They make ideal gifts for teachers or neighbors at Christmas, housewarming treats for friends or "thank you" gifts for host families when you travel.

APRICOT JAM

A pretty jam. Good tasting as well!

Fresh apricots, halved and pitted	**2 lbs.**	**900 g**
Lemon juice	**¼ cup**	**60 mL**
Pectin crystals	**1 x 2 oz.**	**1 x 57 g**
Granulated sugar	**6 cups**	**1.5 L**
Almond flavoring (optional)	**¼ tsp.**	**1 mL**

Grind apricots using coarse blade of food processor. Place in large stock pot.

Add lemon juice and pectin. Heat and stir until mixture boils very rapidly.

Mix in sugar. Stir to dissolve. Return to a full boil. Boil hard for 4 minutes. Add almond flavoring. Skim off foam. Fill hot sterilized half pint jars to within ¼ inch (6 mm) of top. Place sterilized metal lids on jars and screw metal bands on securely. For added assurance against spoilage, you may choose to process in a boiling water bath for 5 minutes. Makes 6 half pints (6 cups,1.5 L).

2 tbsp. (30 mL): *105 Calories; 0.1 g Total Fat; trace Sodium; trace Protein; 27 g Carbohydrate; trace Dietary Fiber*

WHIPPED RASPBERRY JAM

Clear and fresh tasting.

Fresh raspberries	**4 cups**	**1 L**
Granulated sugar	**4 cups**	**1 L**

Place raspberries in large saucepan or Dutch oven. Using potato masher, mash well. Stir until it comes to a boil. Boil rapidly for 2 minutes.

Add sugar. Return to a boil, stirring continually. Boil rapidly for 2 minutes. Remove from heat. Beat on medium for 4 minutes. Fill hot sterilized half pint jars to within ¼ inch (6 mm) of top. Place sterilized metal lids on jars and screw metal bands on securely. For added assurance against spoilage, you may choose to process in a boiling water bath for 5 minutes. Makes 3 half pints plus 1 small jar (3¼ cups, 800 L).

2 tbsp. (30 mL): *129 Calories; 0.1 g Total Fat; trace Sodium; trace Protein; 33 g Carbohydrate; 1 g Dietary Fiber*

Pictured on page 71.

1. Peach Conserve, page 65
2. Peach Butter, page 55
3. Zucchini Marmalade, page 76
4. Whipped Raspberry Jam, page 70
5. Cinnamon Toast Spread, page 86
6. Carrot Marmalade, page 79
7. Mint Jelly, page 75
8. Purple Wine Jelly, page 74

Props Courtesy Of:
Chintz & Company, Creations By Design, Dansk Gifts, Eaton's The Basket House, The Bay

Jellies

hese savory and sweet jellies are so versatile! Whether spread on a morning bagel or poured over a block of cream cheese and spooned onto crackers, these jewel-colored jellies are a delightful treat. Try *Raspberry Jelly* as a topping for custard or *Mint Jelly* served with lamb or over vanilla ice cream. *Hot Pepper Jelly* or *Jalapeño Jelly* is perfect to spice up your party!

HOT PEPPER JELLY

This makes a greenish-colored jelly. Use red peppers to make an orange-red color. Great over a block of cream cheese served with crackers.

Chopped green or red pepper	1½ **cups**	375 mL
Canned chopped jalapeño peppers (see Note)	¼ **cup**	60 mL
White vinegar	1½ **cups**	375 mL
Granulated sugar	6½ **cups**	1.6 L
Liquid pectin	6 oz.	170 mL
Green food coloring (optional)		

Combine peppers and vinegar in blender. Process until smooth. Pour into large stock pot.

Add sugar. Heat and stir until sugar is dissolved. Bring to a boil. Boil for 3 minutes.

Stir in pectin. Return to a full rolling boil. Boil hard for 1 minute. Remove from heat. Skim off foam.

Add bit of food coloring if desired to make a stronger green. Pour into hot sterilized half pint jars to within ¼ inch (6 mm) of top. Place sterilized metal lids on jars and screw metal bands on securely. For added assurance against spoilage, you may choose to process in a boiling water bath for 5 minutes. Makes 6 half pints (6 cups, 1.5 L).

2 tbsp. (30 mL): 107 Calories; trace Total Fat; 11 mg Sodium; trace Protein; 28 g Carbohydrate; trace Dietary Fiber

Note: More fresh or canned jalapeño peppers can be used to make jelly hotter.

APPLE JELLY

A mild glistening jelly that is easy to make without adding pectin.

Tart apples (such as Granny Smith)	4½ lbs.	2 kg
Water	7 cups	1.75 L
Apple juice	5 cups	1.25 L
Lemon juice	3 tbsp.	50 mL
Granulated sugar	5 cups	1.25 L

Remove stems and blossom ends from apples. Coarsely chop apples (peel and cores included). Turn into large stock pot. Add water. Bring to a boil. Cook for about 50 minutes until mushy-soft. Pour into jelly bag and strain over large bowl for several hours or overnight.

Combine apple juice and lemon juice in Dutch oven. Add sugar. Stir until mixture comes to a full rolling boil. Boil hard for about 40 minutes, stirring once or twice. Cool teaspoonful on chilled saucer to see if it jells. If mixture doesn't jell, return to heat for 2 minutes and test again. Repeat until jelly stage has been reached. Skim off foam. Pour into hot sterilized half pint jars to within ¼ inch (6 mm) of top. Place sterilized metal lids on jars and screw metal bands on securely. For added assurance against spoilage, you may choose to process in a boiling water bath for 5 minutes. Makes 3 half pints (3 cups, 750 mL).

2 tbsp. (30 mL): 206 Calories; 0.3 g Total Fat; trace Sodium; trace Protein; 53 g Carbohydrate; 1 g Dietary Fiber

CRABAPPLE JELLY: Use crabapples instead of apples.

JALAPEÑO JELLY

Hahl-ah-PAIN-yoh jelly is different and a treat to eat.

Canned chopped pickled jalapeño peppers (or more)	¼ cup	60 mL
Chopped red pepper	¾ cup	175 mL
White vinegar	1 cup	250 mL
Lemon juice	3 tbsp.	50 mL
Granulated sugar	5 cups	1.25 L
Liquid pectin	3 oz.	85 mL

Put jalapeño and red pepper into blender. Add ½ of vinegar. Process until smooth. Pour into large stock pot. Add remaining ½ of vinegar plus lemon juice and sugar. Bring to a boil. Boil for 1 minute. Remove from heat. Skim off foam. Pour into hot sterilized half pint jars to within ¼ inch (6 mm) of top. Place sterilized metal lids on jars and screw metal bands on securely. For added assurance against spoilage, you may choose to process in a boiling water bath for 5 minutes. Makes 4 half pints (4 cups, 1 L).

2 tbsp. (30 mL): 124 Calories; trace Total Fat; 16 mg Sodium; trace Protein; 32 g Carbohydrate; trace Dietary Fiber

Pictured on page 17.

Pectin is a natural jelling agent found in fruits. Some fruits, such as apples, cranberries, plums and most citrus fruits, have higher levels than apricots, strawberries, raspberries and peaches. If a fruit is overripe or if its natural level of pectin is low, commercial pectin can be added.

WINE JELLY

Tastes like your favorite wine. Makes a different gift.

Red wine (your favorite, not too sweet)	4 cups	1 L
Granulated sugar	6 cups	1.5 L
Liquid pectin	6 oz.	170 mL

Combine wine and sugar in large stock pot. Heat, stirring occasionally, as mixture comes to a rolling boil.

Add pectin. Return to a rolling boil. Boil hard for 1 minute. Skim off foam. Pour into hot sterilized half pint jars to within ¼ inch (6 mm) of top. Place sterilized metal lids on jars and screw metal bands on securely. For added assurance against spoilage, you may choose to process in a boiling water bath for 5 minutes. Makes 8 half pints (8 cups, 2 L).

2 tbsp. (30 mL): 84 Calories; 0 g Total Fat; 1 mg Sodium; trace Protein; 19 g Carbohydrate; 0 g Dietary Fiber

GOLDEN WINE JELLY: Use pale sherry instead of red wine.

PORT WINE JELLY: Use port instead of red wine. Makes a gorgeous ruby-red color.

PURPLE WINE JELLY: Use concord grape wine instead of red wine.

Pictured on page 71.

RASPBERRY JELLY

Clear and ruby red. Perfect spread on toast. Also a good custard topping.

Raspberries (about 5 pint baskets)	10 cups	2.5 L
Pectin crystals	1 × 2 oz.	1 × 57 g
Granulated sugar	5 cups	1.25 L

Place raspberries in large stock pot. Mash with potato masher. Heat just enough to warm a bit so juice runs better. Pour into jelly bag and strain over large bowl. Pour 4 cups (1 L) juice into large stock pot.

Stir in pectin crystals. Stir together until mixture boils.

Add sugar. Stir until mixture boils again. Bring to a full rolling boil. Boil for 4 minutes. Remove from heat. Skim off foam. Pour into hot sterilized half pint jars to within ¼ inch (6 mm) of top. Place sterilized metal lids on jars and screw metal bands on securely. For added assurance against spoilage, you may choose to process in a boiling water bath for 5 minutes. Makes 6 half pints (6 cups, 1.5 L).

2 tbsp. (30 mL): 94 Calories; 0.1 g Total Fat; trace Sodium; trace Protein; 24 g Carbohydrate; 1 g Dietary Fiber

Make your own jelly bag by placing a double layer of cheesecloth or a piece of cotton muslin over a large bowl. Pour fruit with juice onto cloth. Gather top of cloth around fruit and tie tightly with string. Suspend above the bowl by attaching string to cupboard door handle.

MINT JELLY

A good set to this pretty jelly. Serve with lamb. Also good with ice cream.

Tart apples (such as Granny Smith), with peel, cut up	4½ lbs.	2 kg
Water	2 cups	500 mL
Chopped fresh mint, lightly packed (see Note)	1½ cups	375 mL
White vinegar	2 cups	500 mL
Granulated sugar, approximately (see Note)	4 cups	1 L
Drops green food coloring (optional)	3-5	3-5

Combine apple pieces, water and mint in large saucepan. Bring to a boil. Cook until apples are mushy.

Add vinegar. Return to a boil. Boil, covered, for 5 minutes. Pour into jelly bag and strain over large bowl. Measure then pour juice into large stock pot.

Add the same amount of sugar as juice. Heat and stir until sugar is dissolved and a full rolling boil is reached. Add food coloring if desired. Boil rapidly for 25 to 30 minutes. Cool teaspoonful on chilled saucer to see if it jells. If mixture doesn't jell, return to heat for 2 minutes and test again. Repeat until jelly stage has been reached. Pour into hot sterilized half pint jars to within ¼ inch (6 mm) of top. Place sterilized metal lids on jars and screw metal bands on securely. For added assurance against spoilage, you may choose to process in a boiling water bath for 5 minutes. Makes 4 half pints (4 cups, 1 L).

Note: Taste juice before adding sugar. If not minty enough, add 2 or 3 sprigs of mint along with sugar. Discard mint before filling jars.

2 tbsp. (30 mL): 133 Calories; 0.2 g Total Fat; 1 mg Sodium; trace Protein; 34 g Carbohydrate; 1 g Dietary Fiber

Pictured on page 71.

Serve jams, jellies and marmalades in decorative glass jars or containers so that guests can appreciate the beautiful translucence of the contents in the morning light. Offer a good variety of colors and tastes to breakfast or tea guests.

Marmalades

othing captures the essence of summer quite like marmalade. Thin slices of orange and lemon or tart chunks of rhubarb combine to create a zesty spread for the breakfast table. A flavorful and economical way to use up that abundance of rhubarb, carrots and zucchini from the garden.

ZUCCHINI MARMALADE

Economical and flavorful.

Zucchini, peeled, cut up and seeded	6 lbs.	2.7 kg
Granulated sugar	12 cups	3 L
Oranges, with peel	3	3
Lemons, with peel	2	2
Crystallized ginger	2 oz.	57 g

Put zucchini through food grinder into large bowl.

Pour sugar over top. Cover. Let stand on counter overnight. In morning, transfer to large stock pot.

Cut oranges and lemons into wedges. Remove seeds. Put through food grinder. Grind ginger. Add ground ingredients to zucchini mixture. Stir together until sugar is dissolved. Bring to a boil, stirring occasionally. Boil until thickened, stirring occasionally. This will take $1\frac{1}{4}$ hours. Remove from heat. Cool teaspoonful on chilled saucer to see if it jells. If mixture doesn't jell, return to heat for 2 minutes and test again. Repeat until jelly stage has been reached. Fill hot sterilized half pint jars to within $\frac{1}{4}$ inch (6 mm) of top. Place sterilized metal lids on jars and screw metal bands on securely. For added assurance against spoilage, you may choose to process in a boiling water bath for 5 minutes. Makes 12 half pints (12 cups, 3 L).

2 tbsp. (30 mL): 105 Calories; 0.1 g Total Fat; 2 mg Sodium; trace Protein; 27 g Carbohydrate; 1 g Dietary Fiber

Pictured on page 71.

ORANGE MARMALADE

Clear, dark marmalade with slender strips of orange peel throughout.

Medium oranges	6	6
Medium lemons	3	3
Water	3 cups	750 mL
Orange peel		
Lemon peel		
Water	2¼ cups	560 mL
Granulated sugar, approximately	3¼ cups	800 mL

Peel oranges and lemons very thinly trying not to have any white pith on peel. Place peel in plastic bag to keep from drying out. Set aside until morning. Slice oranges and lemons into large stock pot. Add first amount of water. Boil gently for 2 hours. Pour into jelly bag and strain over large bowl overnight.

Cut peel with knife or scissors into fine long shreds. Put into medium saucepan. Add second amount of water. Boil for 15 minutes, stirring occasionally, until soft. Drain and measure 2 cups (500 mL) juice, adding bit of water if needed. Add to juice from jelly bag.

Mix and measure peel and juice, then place in large saucepan. Add same amount of sugar to juice and peel. Stir together until mixture boils. Boil rapidly, stirring 2 or 3 times, until teaspoonful jells when cooled on chilled saucer. This will take about 25 minutes. If mixture doesn't jell, return to heat for 2 minutes and test again. Repeat until jelly stage has been reached. Pour into hot sterilized half pint jars to within ¼ inch (6 mm) of top. Place sterilized metal lids on jars and screw metal bands on securely. For added assurance against spoilage, you may choose to process in a boiling water bath for 5 minutes. Makes 3 half pints plus 1 small jar (3¼ cups, 800 mL).

2 tbsp. (30 mL): 114 Calories; 0.1 g Total Fat; 1 mg Sodium; trace Protein; 29 g Carbohydrate, 1 g Dietary Fiber

GOLDEN RHUBARB MARMALADE

Good taste and texture. A hint of orange.

Chopped fresh rhubarb	8 cups	2 L
Granulated sugar	10 cups	2.5 L
Oranges, put through food grinder	3	3
Lemon, put through food grinder	1	1

Combine all 4 ingredients in large bowl. Stir together. Cover. Let stand overnight on counter. Turn into large stock pot. Bring to a boil, stirring often. Boil for 30 minutes. Cool teaspoonful on chilled saucer to see if it jells. If mixture doesn't jell, return to heat for 2 minutes and test again. Repeat until jelly stage has been reached. Fill hot sterilized half pint jars to within ¼ inch (6 mm) of top. Place sterilized metal lids on jars and screw metal bands on securely. For added assurance against spoilage, you may choose to process in a boiling water bath for 5 minutes. Makes 10 half pints (10 cups, 2.5 L).

2 tbsp. (30 mL): 102 Calories; 0.1 g Total Fat; 1 mg Sodium; trace Protein; 27 g Carbohydrate; 1 g Dietary Fiber

---

When making marmalade, choose fruit with peel that is a deep, even color if possible; it will enhance the appearance of your final product.

GINGER PEAR MARMALADE

Perfect combination.

Peeled, cored and sliced pears, about 4½ lbs. (2 kg)	10 cups	2.5 L
Grated peel and juice of 1 orange		
Grated peel and juice of 1 lemon		
Granulated sugar	6 cups	1.5 L
Piece of gingerroot, about 2 inch (5 cm) length, tied in double layer of cheesecloth		

Combine all 5 ingredients in large saucepan. Stir together. Let stand for about 1 hour until pears release their juice. Heat and stir until mixture comes to a boil. Boil, stirring often, until pears are mushy. Boil rapidly, stirring constantly, until jelly stage is reached. This will take about 55 minutes. If mixture doesn't jell, return to heat for 2 minutes and test again. Repeat until jelly stage has been reached. Discard spice bag. Skim off foam. Fill hot sterilized half pint jars to within ¼ inch (6 mm) of top. Place sterilized metal lids on jars and screw metal bands on securely. For added assurance against spoilage, you may choose to process in a boiling water bath for 5 minutes. Makes 6 half pints (6 cups, 1.5 L).

2 tbsp. (30 mL): 119 Calories; 0.1 g Total Fat; trace Sodium; trace Protein; 31 g Carbohydrate; 1 g Dietary Fiber

RHUBARB MARMALADE

Good taste and texture. Orange flavor comes through.

Fresh rhubarb, cut up	2 lbs.	900 g
Granulated sugar	2 lbs.	900 g
Oranges	1½	1½

Put rhubarb and sugar into large stock pot. Remove very thin layer of orange peel with no white pith on it. Remove and discard white pith from peeled oranges. Slice peel into very thin strips. Cut strips into short lengths. Cut oranges into small pieces. Add peel and pulp to pot. Stir and bring to a boil. Boil, stirring occasionally, for about 30 minutes. Remove from heat. Cool teaspoonful on chilled saucer to see if it jells. If mixture doesn't jell, return to heat for 2 minutes and test again. Repeat until jelly stage has been reached. Fill hot sterilized half pint jars to within ¼ inch (6 mm) of top. Place sterilized metal lids on jars and screw metal bands on securely. For added assurance against spoilage, you may choose to process in a boiling water bath for 5 minutes. Makes 5 half pints (5 cups, 1.25 L).

2 tbsp. (30 mL): 90 Calories; 0.1 g Total Fat; 1 mg Sodium; trace Protein; 23 g Carbohydrate; 1 g Dietary Fiber

ORANGE PINEAPPLE MARMALADE

Any time is preserving time with this easy recipe. It's a snap to make and is destined to be your favorite marmalade.

Large oranges	4	4
Water	2 cups	500 mL
Granulated sugar	4 cups	1 L
Canned crushed pineapple, with juice	2 x 14 oz.	2 x 398 mL

Grate peel from oranges. Put peel and water into medium saucepan. Use orange for another purpose. Bring mixture to a boil. Cover. Simmer for 5 to 10 minutes until peel is soft. Strain juice into large stock pot.

Add sugar and pineapple. Bring to a boil, stirring often. Boil rapidly for about 35 minutes, stirring 2 or 3 times, until thickened. Cool teaspoonful on chilled saucer to see if it jells. If mixture doesn't jell, return to heat for 2 minutes and test again. Repeat until jelly stage has been reached. Fill hot sterilized half pint jars to within 1/4 inch (6 mm) of top. Place sterilized metal lids on jars and screw metal bands on securely. For added assurance against spoilage, you may choose to process in a boiling water bath for 5 minutes. Makes 3 half pints plus 1 small jar (3 1/4 cups, 800 mL).

2 tbsp. (30 mL): 149 Calories; 0.1 g Total Fat; 1 mg Sodium; 1 g Protein; 40 g Carbohydrate; 2 g Dietary Fiber

CARROT MARMALADE

Lots of body to this. Very pretty color.

Grated carrot, about 2 lbs. (900 g)	6 cups	1.5 L
Lemons, with peel, seeded and ground	1 1/2	1 1/2
Oranges, with peel, seeded and ground	1 1/2	1 1/2
Canned crushed pineapple, with juice	1 cup	250 mL
Granulated sugar	6 cups	1.5 L
Salt	1/2 tsp.	2 mL
Chopped maraschino cherries, drained	1/3 cup	75 mL

Mix first 6 ingredients in large bowl. Cover. Let stand overnight on counter. Transfer to large stock pot. Bring to a boil, stirring frequently. Boil rapidly for 3 minutes without stirring.

Add cherries. Stir together. Fill hot sterilized half pint jars to within 1/4 inch (6 mm) of top. Place sterilized metal lids on jars and screw metal bands on securely. For added assurance against spoilage, you may choose to process in a boiling water bath for 5 minutes. Makes 8 half pints (8 cups, 2 L).

2 tbsp. (30 mL): 83 Calories; trace Total Fat; 24 mg Sodium; trace Protein; 22 g Carbohydrate; 1 g Dietary Fiber

Pictured on page 71.

For practical as well as aesthetic reasons, serve jam, jelly or marmalade in a small crock with its own tiny spoon. This way, the knife covered with toast crumbs won't find its way back into the jar.

PEACH ORANGE MARMALADE

A gorgeous shade of reddish orange. Excellent flavor.

Peaches, with peel, pitted and quartered	7	7
Orange, cut up and seeds removed	1	1
Maraschino cherries, drained	1/3 cup	75 mL
Granulated sugar, approximately	4 cups	1 L
Almond flavoring	1/2 tsp.	2 mL

Put peach, orange and cherries through food grinder. Measure pulp and turn into large stock pot.

Add same amount of sugar as there is pulp. Add almond flavoring. Heat and stir together until sugar is dissolved and mixture comes to a boil. Boil for 30 to 40 minutes, stirring occasionally, until teaspoonful cooled on chilled saucer jells. If mixture doesn't jell, return to heat for 2 minutes and test again. Repeat until jelly stage has been reached. Fill hot sterilized half pint jars to within 1/4 inch (6 mm) of top. Place sterilized metal lids on jars and screw metal bands on securely. For added assurance against spoilage, you may choose to process in a boiling water bath for 5 minutes. Makes 5 half pints (5 cups, 1.25 L).

2 tbsp. (30 mL): 87 Calories; trace Total Fat; trace Sodium; trace Protein; 23 g Carbohydrate; 1 g Dietary Fiber

THREE FRUIT MARMALADE

Very good flavor. Makes a large batch but may be halved. Not a real firm marmalade.

Grapefruit, with peel, cut up	1/2	1/2
Orange, with peel, quartered	1	1
Lemon, with peel, halved	1	1
Water, 3 times amount of fruit		
Granulated sugar, approximately 1 1/2 times quantity of pulp	3 cups	750 mL

Remove seeds from grapefruit, orange and lemon. Put through food grinder. Measure and put into large saucepan.

For each 1 cup (250 mL) pulp, add 3 cups (750 mL) water. Bring to a boil, stirring occasionally. Simmer for 20 minutes. Boil rapidly, stirring 2 or 3 times, for 20 minutes. Measure quantity.

To each 1 cup (250 mL) pulp, add 1 1/2 cups (375 mL) sugar. Return to a boil, stirring. Boil rapidly until thickened and teaspoonful cooled on chilled saucer jells. This will take about 20 minutes. If mixture doesn't jell, return to heat for 2 minutes and test again. Repeat until jelly stage has been reached. Fill hot sterilized half pint jars to within 1/4 inch (6 mm) of top. Place sterilized metal lids on jars and screw metal bands on securely. For added assurance against spoilage, you may choose to process in a boiling water bath for 5 minutes. Makes 5 half pints (5 cups, 1.25 L).

2 tbsp. (30 mL): 62 Calories; trace Total Fat; trace Sodium; trace Protein; 16 g Carbohydrate; trace Dietary Fiber

Mousses

Whether it's shrimp, crab, salmon or corned beef, a savory mousse is an elegant dish sure to impress. All of these make-ahead molds are a perfect addition to a buffet table or appetizer menu. Serve these recipes on a bed of lettuce and garnish with parsley or cherry tomato halves. Be creative with an assortment of crackers or toast cups.

CORNED BEEF MOUSSE

An easy-to-make spread that is absolutely luscious.

Envelope unflavored gelatin	1 × ¼ oz.	1 × 7 g
Cold water	¼ cup	60 mL
Condensed cream of mushroom soup	10 oz.	284 mL
Cream cheese, softened	8 oz.	250 g
Curry powder	¼ tsp.	1 mL
Finely chopped onion	½ cup	125 mL
Finely chopped celery	½ cup	125 mL
Salad dressing (or mayonnaise)	1 cup	250 mL
Canned corned beef, flaked	7 oz.	198 g

Sprinkle gelatin over cold water in medium saucepan. Let stand for 5 minutes.

Add mushroom soup, cream cheese and curry powder. Heat and stir until gelatin is dissolved and cream cheese is melted. Remove from heat. Chill until mixture begins to thicken.

Add onion, celery and salad dressing. Fold corned beef into mixture. Pour into 5 cup (1.25 L) mold. Chill. Unmold onto serving plate. Makes about 5 cups (1.25 L).

2 tbsp. (30 mL): 71 Calories; 6.2 g Total Fat; 160 mg Sodium; 2 g Protein; 2 g Carbohydrate; trace Dietary Fiber

Mousse is French for "frothy," and mousses tend to be light and frothy (almost sponge like) in texture. The best mold for a mousse is one made of metal. Because mousses are creamy, use smooth molds without a lot of detail so that the mousse slides out easily.

salmon mousses

Minimal effort is needed to prepare these star attraction mousses. The recipe on the right will allow more servings for those guests who just can't get enough!

★★★★★

Envelope unflavored gelatin	1 x ¼ oz.	1 x 7 g
Cold water	½ cup	125 mL
Salad dressing (or mayonnaise)	½ cup	125 mL
Sour cream	¼ cup	60 mL
Lemon juice	1 tbsp.	15 mL
Dill weed	2 tsp.	10 mL
Onion powder	1 tsp.	5 mL
Paprika	1 tsp.	5 mL
Hot pepper sauce	½ tsp.	2 mL
Salt	¼ tsp.	1 mL
Canned red salmon, drained, skin and round bones removed, flaked	7½ oz.	213 g
Envelope dessert topping (prepared according to package directions)	1	1

Sprinkle gelatin over cold water in small saucepan. Let stand for 1 minute. Heat and stir until gelatin is dissolved. Remove from heat. Cool.

Add next 8 ingredients. Whisk together. Chill, stirring often, until mixture starts to thicken.

Fold in salmon.

Fold dessert topping into salmon mixture. Turn into 4 cup (1 L) mold. Chill. Unmold onto serving plate. Makes 4 cups (1 L).

2 tbsp. (30 mL): 40 Calories; 3.2 g Total Fat; 73 mg Sodium; 1 g Protein; 1 g Carbohydrate; trace Dietary Fiber

Pictured on front cover.

★★★★★

Envelopes unflavored gelatin	2 x ¼ oz.	2 x 7 g
Cold water	1½ cups	375 mL
Non-fat sour cream	1 cup	250 mL
Low-fat salad dressing (or mayonnaise)	1 cup	250 mL
Dill weed	½ tsp.	2 mL
Onion powder	½ tsp.	2 mL
Celery salt	½ tsp.	2 mL
Canned salmon, drained, skin and round bones removed, flaked (red is best for color)	2 x 7½ oz.	2 x 213 g
Finely chopped English cucumber, with peel	1 cup	250 mL

Sprinkle gelatin over cold water in small saucepan. Let stand for at least 1 minute. Heat and stir together until gelatin is dissolved. Remove from heat. Cool.

Mix next 5 ingredients well in large bowl. When gelatin has cooled thoroughly but not thickened, add to sour cream mixture. Mix. Refrigerate, stirring and scraping sides of bowl occasionally.

Fold in salmon and cucumber. Pour into 5 cup (1.25 L) mold. Chill until firm. Unmold onto serving plate. Makes 5 cups (1.25 L).

2 tbsp. (30 mL): 37 Calories; 2.6 g Total Fat; 108 mg Sodium; 2 g Protein; 1 g Carbohydrate; trace Dietary Fiber

CRAB SPREAD

This is a winner every time!

Envelope unflavored gelatin	1 x ¼ oz.	1 x 7 g
Cold water	¼ cup	60 mL
Condensed cream of mushroom soup	10 oz.	284 mL
Cream cheese, cut up	8 oz.	250 g
Chopped chives	1 tsp.	5 mL
Onion powder	¼ tsp.	1 mL
Celery salt	⅛ tsp.	0.5 mL
Salad dressing (or mayonnaise)	2 tbsp.	30 mL
Canned crabmeat, drained and cartilage removed	4.2 oz.	120 g

Sprinkle gelatin over cold water in small cup. Let stand.

Heat next 5 ingredients in medium saucepan, stirring often. When mixture is melted and hot, stir in gelatin mixture to dissolve. Remove from heat.

Add salad dressing and crabmeat. Stir together. Pour into 3 cup (750 mL) ring mold. Chill. Unmold onto serving plate. Makes 3 cups (750 mL).

2 tbsp. (30 mL): 57 Calories; 5 g Total Fat; 172 mg Sodium; 2 g Protein; 1 g Carbohydrate; trace Dietary Fiber

SHRIMP MOUSSE

A real party attraction.

Envelopes unflavored gelatin	2 x ¼ oz.	2 x 7 g
Cold water	½ cup	125 mL
Cream cheese, softened	8 oz.	250 g
Condensed tomato soup	10 oz.	284 mL
Salad dressing (or mayonnaise)	½ cup	125 mL
Lemon juice	2 tbsp.	30 mL
Salt	½ tsp.	2 mL
Onion powder	½ tsp.	2 mL
Worcestershire sauce	¼ tsp.	1 mL
Finely chopped celery	1 cup	250 mL
Finely chopped green pepper	⅓ cup	75 mL
Canned small (or broken) shrimp, drained and chopped	2 x 4 oz.	2 x 113 g

Sprinkle gelatin over cold water in small saucepan. Let stand for 1 minute. Heat and stir until gelatin is dissolved. Remove from heat.

Beat cream cheese and tomato soup together in small bowl until smooth. Beat in salad dressing, lemon juice, salt, onion powder and Worcestershire sauce. Add gelatin mixture. Mix.

Fold in remaining 3 ingredients. Turn into 6 cup (1.5 L) mold. Chill. Unmold onto serving plate. Makes 5½ cups (1.4 L).

2 tbsp. (30 mL): 44 Calories; 3.4 g Total Fat; 119 mg Sodium; 2 g Protein; 1 g Carbohydrate; trace Dietary Fiber

Other Spreads

ll types of spreads are included in this section. For the family, have *Cinnamon Toast Spread* on hand for those fast-paced early morning breakfasts. Enjoy many of the sandwich spreads when having a casual lunch get-together with friends. These sandwich spreads are also great when you need more ideas for school lunches. When planning a party, make your own pâté—smooth or chunky, everyone on your guest list will love a selection of these impressive appetizers.

CHEESE SPREAD

This spread is speckled throughout. Best served at room temperature with crackers, raw vegetables or fruit.

Process cheese spread, room temperature	**1 cup**	**250 mL**
Cream cheese, softened	**12 oz.**	**375 g**
Blue cheese, crumbled and softened	**4 oz.**	**125 g**
Hard margarine (or butter), softened	**¼ cup**	**60 mL**
Finely grated onion	**1 tbsp.**	**15 mL**
Worcestershire sauce	**1 tsp.**	**5 mL**
Garlic powder	**¼ tsp.**	**1 mL**
Ground pecans	**½ cup**	**125 mL**
Chopped fresh parsley (or 2 tsp.,10 mL, flakes)	**¼ cup**	**60 mL**
Ground pecans	**½ cup**	**125 mL**
Chopped fresh parsley (or 2 tsp.,10 mL, flakes)	**¼ cup**	**60 mL**

Place first 9 ingredients in medium bowl. Beat together well. Pack into shallow serving bowl.

Sprinkle with second amounts of pecans and parsley. Makes 3½ cups (875 mL).

2 tbsp. (30 mL): 125 Calories; 11.7 g Total Fat; 266 mg Sodium; 4 g Protein; 2 g Carbohydrate; trace Dietary Fiber

POLYNESIAN CREAM CHEESE

Not only is this quick and easy, but a block of cheese may be cut in half lengthwise to make two varieties.

Cream cheese	**8 oz.**	**250 g**
Soy sauce	**⅓ cup**	**75 mL**
Sesame seed, toasted (see Note)	**1-2 tbsp.**	**15-30 mL**

Put block of cream cheese into small bowl or plastic bag. Pour soy sauce over top. Marinate for 1 hour. Remove cream cheese to serving plate. Pour more soy sauce over if needed.

Sprinkle with seed. Cheese may also be rolled in seeds, using enough to cover. Makes 1⅓ cups (325 mL).

2 tbsp. (30 mL): 89 Calories; 8.3 g Total Fat; 588 mg Sodium; 3 g Protein; 2 g Carbohydrate; trace Dietary Fiber

Note: Toast sesame seed in ungreased shallow dish in 350°F (175°C) oven for about 5 minutes, stirring once.

ORIENTAL CHEESE SPREAD: Marinate in teriyaki sauce or use ½ cup (125 mL) soy sauce and ¼ cup (60 mL) granulated sugar. Roll in ⅓ cup (75 mL) toasted sesame seed. Sprinkle any leftover seed over top.

APRICOT CHEESE SPREAD: Mix ¼ cup (60 mL) apricot jam, ½ tsp. (2 mL) hot pepper sauce and 2 tsp. (10 mL) cider vinegar. Pour over block of cream cheese.

CHUTNEY BACON SPREAD: Put cream cheese in center of pretty plate. Spoon ¼ cup (60 mL) chutney over top, letting it run down sides. Sprinkle with 6 to 8 slices cooked and crumbled bacon.

SAUCED CHEESE SPREAD: Pour your favorite steak sauce over block of cream cheese. Sprinkle with toasted sesame seed if desired.

SHRIMP CHEESE SPREAD: Pour seafood cocktail sauce or chili sauce over block of cream cheese. Arrange small drained shrimp over top.

CRAB CHEESE SPREAD: Mix seafood cocktail sauce or chili sauce with can of crabmeat, cartilage removed. Spoon over block of cream cheese, letting it run down sides.

SEEDED CHEESE SPREAD: Roll cream cheese block in caraway seed, poppy seed or finely chopped walnuts or pecans.

Curry powder is actually a blend of up to 20 ground spices which may include coriander, cardamom, cinnamon, cloves, mustard, black peppercorns, fenugreek, cumin and turmeric. It quickly loses its pungency and so should be stored airtight no longer than two months. Buy small quantities in bulk and replace as needed.

MUSHROOM SPREAD

May also be used as a dip. A bit unusual. A good mock caviar.

Hard margarine (or butter)	2 tbsp.	30 mL
Finely chopped onion	¾ cup	175 mL
Fresh mushrooms, finely chopped	1 cup	250 mL
Paprika	1½ tsp.	7 mL
Sour cream	½ cup	125 mL
Lemon juice	1 tbsp.	15 mL
Salt	¼ tsp.	1 mL
Dill weed	¼ tsp.	1 mL
Pepper, light sprinkle		

Melt margarine in medium frying pan. Add onion. Sauté for 2 to 3 minutes.

Add mushrooms and paprika. Sauté for 3 to 4 minutes.

Stir in sour cream, lemon juice, salt, dill weed and pepper. Makes 1½ cups (375 mL).

2 tbsp. (30 mL): 38 Calories; 3.3 g Total Fat; 81 mg Sodium; 1 g Protein; 2 g Carbohydrate; trace Dietary Fiber

CINNAMON TOAST SPREAD

A real treat. This was a staple in our house for after school snacks and is now my grandchildrens' favorite. Spread about 1 tbsp. (15 mL) on hot slice of toast.

Hard margarine (or butter)	⅓ cup	75 mL
Granulated sugar	⅔ cup	150 mL
Ground cinnamon	1 tbsp.	15 mL

Put all 3 ingredients into small saucepan. Stir together until margarine is melted. Remove saucepan from heat. Cool. Margarine will rise to top. Stir together well and store in container. Makes about ¾ cup (175 mL).

2 tbsp. (30 mL): 182 Calories; 10.4 g Total Fat; 122 mg Sodium; trace Protein; 23 g Carbohydrate; trace Dietary Fiber

Pictured on page 71.

Variation: Combine sugar and cinnamon and sprinkle as much as you like on warm, buttered toast. Store in container.

A block of Parmesan cheese will keep longer than softer cheeses because it contains very little moisture. Wrap airtight in plastic and store in the refrigerator. Change the wrapping every few days to eliminate any moisture and oils. For longer storage or to freeze, wrap in plastic and then rewrap in foil—it will keep for up to two months. Before using, thaw slowly in the refrigerator.

SANDWICH SPREAD

Just tart enough.

Medium green pepper, finely ground	1	1
Medium red pepper, finely ground	1	1
White vinegar	¾ cup	175 mL
Granulated sugar	1 cup	250 mL
Whipping cream	1 cup	250 mL
Hard margarine (or butter)	½ cup	125 mL
Coarse (pickling) salt	2 tsp.	10 mL
Dry mustard	1 tbsp.	15 mL
Large eggs	3	3
All-purpose flour	¼ cup	60 mL
Grated medium Cheddar cheese	1 cup	250 mL

Combine first 8 ingredients in large saucepan. Heat, stirring often, until boiling.

Mix eggs and flour in small bowl until smooth. Stir into boiling mixture until it returns to a boil and thickens.

Stir in cheese until melted. Cool for 15 minutes. Fill freezer containers to within 1 inch (2.5 cm) of top. Cover and freeze. Use within 3 months. Makes 4 to 5 half pints (4 to 5 cups, 1 to 1.25 L).

2 tbsp. (30 mL): 102 Calories; 7.1 g Total Fat; 228 mg Sodium; 2 g Protein; 8 g Carbohydrate; trace Dietary Fiber

---

Because cottage cheese is a soft, fresh cheese it is highly perishable. Be sure and check the expiry date on the container and use up as soon as possible.

COTTAGE DATE SPREAD

A slightly sweet flavor. Good.

Creamed cottage cheese, mashed	½ cup	125 mL
Ground dates	⅓ cup	75 mL
Finely chopped walnuts	¼ cup	60 mL

Mix all 3 ingredients well in small bowl. Makes about ¾ cup (175 mL).

2 tbsp. (30 mL): 71 Calories; 3.5 g Total Fat; 81 mg Sodium; 3 g Protein; 8 g Carbohydrate; 1 g Dietary Fiber

COTTAGE PEPPER SPREAD

Attractive looking spread for toasted bun halves.

Creamed cottage cheese	½ cup	125 mL
Chopped green onion	2 tbsp.	30 mL
Chopped green pepper	2 tbsp.	30 mL
Salt, sprinkle		

Combine all 4 ingredients in small bowl. Makes about ½ cup (125 mL).

2 tbsp. (30 mL): 23 Calories; 0.3 g Total Fat; 121 mg Sodium; 4 g Protein; 1 g Carbohydrate; trace Dietary Fiber

COTTAGE CARROT SPREAD

Delicious.

Creamed cottage cheese, mashed	½ cup	125 mL
Grated carrot	¼ cup	60 mL
Finely chopped walnuts	2 tbsp.	30 mL
Salad dressing (or mayonnaise)	2 tbsp.	30 mL
Salt	¼ tsp.	1 mL

Mix all 5 ingredients in small bowl. Makes about ⅔ cup (150 mL).

2 tbsp. (30 mL): 63 Calories; 4.6 g Total Fat; 247 mg Sodium; 3 g Protein; 2 g Carbohydrate; trace Dietary Fiber

SURPRISE SPREAD

You will be tempted to eat this no-bake spread by the spoonful.

Cream cheese, softened	8 oz.	250 g
Sour cream	½ cup	125 mL
Salad dressing (or mayonnaise)	¼ cup	60 mL
Canned small (or broken shrimp), drained (see Note)	3 x 4 oz.	3 x 113 g
Seafood cocktail sauce	1 cup	250 mL
Shredded mozzarella cheese	2 cups	500 mL
Green pepper, chopped	1	1
Green onions, chopped	3	3
Medium tomato, diced	1	1

Mix first 3 ingredients in small bowl. Spread over 12 inch (30 cm) pizza pan.

Scatter shrimp over cheese mixture. Add layers of seafood sauce, mozzarella cheese, green pepper, green onion and tomato. Cover and chill until ready to serve. Makes 6 cups (1.5 L).

2 tbsp. (30 mL): 58 Calories; 4 g Total Fat; 113 mg Sodium; 3 g Protein; 3 g Carbohydrate; trace Dietary Fiber

Pictured on page 35.

Note: Omit 1 can of shrimp if desired. It will still cover quite well.

BOURSIN

A good imitation of the real thing. Makes a great spread for bagels and crackers.

Cream cheese, softened	8 oz.	250 g
Dried sweet basil	1 tsp.	5 mL
Dill weed	1 tsp.	5 mL
Chopped chives	1 tsp.	5 mL
Garlic salt	½ tsp.	2 mL

Mash all 5 ingredients together well in small bowl with fork. Refrigerate until needed. Makes 1 cup (250 mL).

2 tbsp. (30 mL): 106 Calories; 10.5 g Total Fat; 170 mg Sodium; 2 g Protein; 1 g Carbohydrate; trace Dietary Fiber

1. Chicken Almond Spread, page 94
2. Beef Salad Spread, page 93
3. Butter Nut Spread, page 91
4. Fruit Dip, page 24
5. Dill Dip, page 38
6. Strawberry Cream, page 91

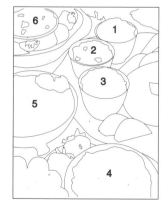

Props Courtesy Of:
Chintz & Company, La Cache, Le Gnome, Scona Clayworks

CREAMED LEMON CHEESE

So scrumptious. Spread over muffins or bread.

Cream cheese, softened	4 oz.	125 g
Lemon juice	1 tbsp.	15 mL
Grated lemon peel	1 tsp.	5 mL

Beat all 3 ingredients together well in small bowl. Makes ½ cup (125 mL).

2 tbsp. (30 mL): 106 Calories; 10.5 g Total Fat; 89 mg Sodium; 1 g Protein; 1 g Carbohydrate; trace Dietary Fiber

CREAM CHEESE SPREAD

A sweet touch to this one.

Cream cheese, softened	4 oz.	125 g
Hard margarine (or butter), softened	2 tbsp.	30 mL
Vanilla	¾ tsp.	4 mL
Icing (confectioner's) sugar	¾ cup	175 mL
Finely chopped pecans	¼ cup	60 mL

Beat cream cheese, margarine, vanilla and icing sugar together well in medium bowl. Stir in pecans. Makes 1 cup (250 mL).

2 tbsp. (30 mL): 143 Calories; 10.6 g Total Fat; 77 mg Sodium; 1 g Protein; 11 g Carbohydrate; trace Dietary Fiber

ORANGE CREAM SPREAD

Use to spread on date, pumpkin, raisin, apple, ginger, orange and peanut butter loaves.

Cream cheese, softened	4 oz.	125 g
Frozen concentrated orange juice	3 tbsp.	50 mL
Granulated sugar	1 tbsp.	15 mL

Mix all 3 ingredients in small bowl until smooth. Makes ¾ cup (175 mL).

2 tbsp. (30 mL): 91 Calories; 7 g Total Fat; 59 mg Sodium; 2 g Protein; 6 g Carbohydrate; trace Dietary Fiber

ORANGE BAGEL SPREAD

Spread over your favorite bagels.

Light (or regular) cream cheese, softened	4 oz.	125 g
Orange marmalade	2 tbsp.	30 mL

Mash cream cheese and marmalade together in small bowl. Makes generous ½ cup (125 mL).

2 tbsp. (30 mL): 87 Calories; 5 g Total Fat; 287 mg Sodium; 3 g Protein; 8 g Carbohydrate; trace Dietary Fiber

Pictured on front cover.

CHOCOLATE BAGEL SPREAD: Mash 4 oz. (125 g) softened cream cheese, ¼ cup (60 mL) sweetened chocolate drink powder and ½ tsp. (2 mL) granulated sugar together in small bowl. Makes ½ cup (125 mL).

FRUIT SPREAD

A slight tang to this. Great on sliced loaves or coffee cakes.

Cream cheese, softened	4 oz.	125 g
Medium orange, with peel, quartered and seeds removed	1	1
Raisins	2 cups	500 mL
Pecans	1 cup	250 mL
Salad dressing (or mayonnaise)	¼ cup	60 mL

Combine all 5 ingredients in food processor until almost smooth. If you don't have a food processor, grind orange, raisins and pecans first. Mix with cream cheese and salad dressing. Makes 2½ cups (625 mL).

2 tbsp. (30 mL): 120 Calories; 7.4 g Total Fat; 38 mg Sodium; 1 g Protein; 14 g Carbohydrate; 1 g Dietary Fiber

BUTTER NUT SPREAD

Lightly toasting the hazelnuts will enhance the flavor. Use any kind of nut you have on hand.

Butter (or hard margarine), softened	½ cup	125 mL
Grated orange peel	1 tbsp.	15 mL
Hazelnuts, finely chopped	½ cup	125 mL

Beat margarine in small bowl until fluffy. Mix in orange peel and hazelnuts. Makes 1 cup (250 mL).

2 tbsp. (30 mL): 152 Calories; 16.3 g Total Fat; 138 mg Sodium; 1 g Protein; 1 g Carbohydrate; 1 g Dietary Fiber

Pictured on page 89.

STRAWBERRY CREAM

Sweet, refreshing and very easy.

Cream cheese, softened	4 oz.	125 g
Strawberry jam	¼-½ cup	60-125 mL

Beat both ingredients together well in small bowl. Makes ¾ cup (175 mL).

2 tbsp. (30 mL): 107 Calories; 7 g Total Fat; 61 mg Sodium; 2 g Protein; 10 g Carbohydrate; 1 g Dietary Fiber

Pictured on page 89.

CURRIED CHEESE SPREAD

Delicious. Serve with butter knife and crackers. Good on just about anything!

Cream cheese, softened	8 oz.	250 g
Apricot jam	¼ cup	60 mL
Chopped almonds (or cashews), toasted (see Note)	⅓ cup	75 mL
Curry powder	¼-½ tsp.	1-2 mL
Dry mustard	¼ tsp.	1 mL

Mash cream cheese and jam together in medium bowl.

Mix in almonds, curry powder and dry mustard. Add smaller amount of curry powder first then more if needed. Pack in small bowl. Makes about 1¼ cups (300 mL).

2 tbsp. (30 mL): 133 Calories; 10.8 g Total Fat; 72 mg Sodium; 3 g Protein; 8 g Carbohydrate; 1 g Dietary Fiber

Note: To toast almonds, place in single layer in pie plate. Bake in 350°F (175°C) oven for 10 to 15 minutes until browned.

CURRIED CHEDDAR SPREAD: Substitute 2 cups (500 mL) grated sharp Cheddar cheese for cream cheese.

CHUTNEY SPREAD: Substitute chutney for apricot jam.

Cream cheese has become a popular staple. A most versatile ingredient when cooking or baking, it is delicious as-is or as a base for more elaborate spreads. Light, non-fat, spreadable and even flavored cream cheeses are available, and can be used interchangeably in recipes with a slight variance in taste. If reheating, low-fat or non-fat products may be much runnier or may separate.

PEANUT RAISIN SPREAD

Rich and creamy. Perfect on toast or crackers.

Smooth peanut butter	½ cup	125 mL
Chopped raisins	½ cup	125 mL
Chopped celery	½ cup	125 mL
Salad dressing (or mayonnaise)	2-3 tbsp.	30-50 mL

Stir first 3 ingredients together in small bowl, adding more salad dressing to taste as well as for moisture. Makes about 1½ cups (375 mL).

2 tbsp. (30 mL): 95 Calories; 6.6 g Total Fat; 72 mg Sodium; 3 g Protein; 8 g Carbohydrate; 1 g Dietary Fiber

PEANUT CARROT SPREAD

Peanut flavor is mild. Delicious on orange or date bread.

Smooth peanut butter	½ cup	125 mL
Grated carrot	½ cup	125 mL
Salad dressing (or mayonnaise)	2 tbsp.	30 mL
Lemon juice	½ tsp.	2 mL

Stir all 4 ingredients together in small bowl. Makes about 1 cup (250 mL).

2 tbsp. (30 mL): 78 Calories; 6.6 g Total Fat; 68 mg Sodium; 2 g Protein; 4 g Carbohydrate; 1 g Dietary Fiber

NUTTY CHEESE SPREAD

Ever popular Cheddar served with a crunch. Tasty and nutty.

Grated Cheddar cheese	1 cup	250 mL
Chopped walnuts	⅔ cup	150 mL
Parsley flakes	2 tsp.	10 mL
Onion flakes, crushed	2 tsp.	10 mL
Salad dressing (or mayonnaise)	½ cup	125 mL

Mix all 5 ingredients together in medium bowl. Makes about 1 cup (250 mL).

2 tbsp. (30 mL): 201 Calories; 18.6 g Total Fat; 183 mg Sodium; 5 g Protein; 5 g Carbohydrate; 1 g Dietary Fiber

HAM SPREAD

Very fast and convenient.

Canned flakes of ham	6½ oz.	184 g
Sweet pickle relish	1 tbsp.	15 mL
Onion flakes, crushed	½ tsp.	2 mL
Salad dressing (or mayonnaise)	4 tsp.	20 mL

Mash all 4 ingredients together in small bowl, adding bit more salad dressing if too dry. Makes ½ cup (125 mL).

2 tbsp. (30 mL): 133 Calories; 10.7 g Total Fat; 648 mg Sodium; 7 g Protein; 2 g Carbohydrate; trace Dietary Fiber

Pictured on page 35.

When entertaining, pass around a wicker basket filled with a variety of bagels, croissants, pitas and whole-grain buns, all cut in half. Offer several different spreads (try fish, egg and ham), each with its own spreader knife, and let your guests mix and match spreads and breads. Complete the setting with a tray of pickles, lettuce leaves and tomato slices.

EGG SALAD SPREAD

A favorite among the egg salad sandwich fans.

Hard-boiled eggs, chopped	6	6
Diced peeled cucumber, seeded and drained	1 cup	250 mL
Diced celery	1 cup	250 mL
Chopped green onion	3 tbsp.	50 mL
Chopped pimiento	2 tbsp.	30 mL
Salt	1 tsp.	5 mL
Salad dressing (or mayonnaise)	½ cup	125 mL

Mix all 7 ingredients in medium bowl. Makes about 3 cups (750 mL).

2 tbsp. (30 mL): 45 Calories; 3.7 g Total Fat; 159 mg Sodium; 2 g Protein; 1 g Carbohydrate; trace Dietary Fiber

Pictured on page 35.

EGG CHEESE SPREAD

Use mild, medium or sharp Cheddar cheese.

Hard-boiled eggs, chopped	4	4
Cheddar cheese, cubed	1 cup	250 mL
Small onion, cut up	1	1
Salt	½ tsp.	2 mL
Pepper	¼ tsp.	1 mL

Process or grind all 5 ingredients. Add some melted margarine to moisten if needed. Makes about 2⅓ cups (575 mL).

2 tbsp. (30 mL): 42 Calories; 3.1 g Total Fat; 121 mg Sodium; 3 g Protein; 1 g Carbohydrate; trace Dietary Fiber

──────

Traditional egg spreads are not only delicious but also nourishing. Use as a filling between celery sticks, stuffed into zucchini "boats", or spread between two apple halves.

BEEF SALAD SPREAD

A good way to use up leftover roast beef.

Ground cooked roast beef	2 cups	500 mL
Chopped celery	1 cup	250 mL
Chopped onion	2 tbsp.	30 mL
Sweet pickle relish	2 tbsp.	30 mL
Salt	½ tsp.	2 mL
Pepper	⅛ tsp.	0.5 mL
Salad dressing (or mayonnaise)	¼ cup	60 mL
Lemon juice	1 tbsp.	15 mL

Mix all 8 ingredients in medium bowl. Makes about 2½ cups (625 mL).

2 tbsp. (30 mL): 42 Calories; 2.2 g Total Fat; 104 mg Sodium; 4 g Protein; 1 g Carbohydrate; trace Dietary Fiber

Pictured on page 89.

CORNED BEEF SPREAD

With ingredients on hand, this seldom-thought of meat works wonders. Spread on rye bread, pumpernickel or crackers.

Canned corned beef, mashed	12 oz.	340 g
Hard-boiled eggs, chopped	2	2
Salad dressing (or mayonnaise)	½ cup	125 mL
Onion flakes	2 tsp.	10 mL
Water	2 tsp.	10 mL
Worcestershire sauce	1 tsp.	5 mL

Mix corned beef and eggs in medium bowl.

Combine next 4 ingredients in small bowl. Stir together. Add to corned beef mixture. Mix. Makes about 2½ cups (625 mL).

2 tbsp. (30 mL): 79 Calories; 5.9 g Total Fat; 210 mg Sodium; 5 g Protein; 1 g Carbohydrate; trace Dietary Fiber

CHICKEN ALMOND SPREAD

A good nutty spread.

Ground cooked chicken	2 cups	500 mL
Toasted ground almonds (see Note)	¾ cup	175 mL
Salad dressing (or mayonnaise)	½ cup	125 mL
Parsley flakes	1 tsp.	5 mL
Seasoning salt	1 tsp.	5 mL

Mix all 5 ingredients well in medium bowl, adding up to ¼ cup (60 mL) more salad dressing to taste. Milk may be added if too dry. Makes about 1½ cups (375 mL).

2 tbsp. (30 mL): 141 Calories; 9.5 g Total Fat; 195 mg Sodium; 11 g Protein; 3 g Carbohydrate; 1 g Dietary Fiber

Pictured on page 89.

Note: To toast almonds, place in single layer in pie plate. Bake in 350°F (175°C) oven for 10 to 15 minutes until browned.

CHICKEN CURRY SPREAD: Add about ½ tsp. (2 mL) curry powder to Chicken Almond Spread.

CHICKEN SALAD SPREAD

This will be a favorite at family picnics.

Ground cooked chicken	2 cups	500 mL
Chopped celery	½ cup	125 mL
Salt	¾ tsp.	3 mL
Lemon juice	1 tsp.	5 mL
Salad dressing (or mayonnaise)	½ cup	125 mL
Parsley flakes	1 tsp.	5 mL
Onion powder	¼ tsp.	1 mL

Mix all 7 ingredients in medium bowl. Check for seasoning. Makes about 1½ cups (375 mL).

2 tbsp. (30 mL): 103 Calories; 6 g Total Fat; 253 mg Sodium; 10 g Protein; 2 g Carbohydrate; trace Dietary Fiber

FOOTBALL PÂTÉ

This quick pâté is a blessing to busy holidayers. The flavor is excellent. Make the day before.

Hard margarine (or butter)	⅓ cup	75 mL
Chopped fresh mushrooms	2 cups	500 mL
Chopped onion	1 cup	250 mL
Liverwurst spread (or liverwurst sausage)	24 oz.	750 g
Brandy flavoring	1 tsp.	5 mL
Onion powder	½ tsp.	2 mL
Peppercorns and pimiento, for garnish		

Melt margarine in large frying pan. Add mushrooms and onion. Sauté until onion is clear and soft and mixture is fairly dry of moisture.

Stir in next 3 ingredients. Put into large bowl. Chill. Remove from bowl. Shape into football. Place on tray. Cover and chill until needed.

Garnish with peppercorns and strips of pimiento to resemble a football. Makes about 5 cups (1.25 L).

2 tbsp. (30 mL): 75 Calories; 6.7 g Total Fat; 173 mg Sodium; 2 g Protein; trace Carbohydrate; 1 g Dietary Fiber

Pâté is French for "pie." Traditionally it is a rich well-seasoned finely ground meat mixture packed into a terrine or turned out and served as a pâté. Serve with a small spreader and rounds of dark bread and wheat crackers. Pâtés make an elegant pre-dinner appetizer or can round out your evening appetizer selections.

LIVER PÂTÉ

Simple to prepare, a tasty spread. Serve with cocktail crackers.

Chicken livers	¾ lb.	340 g
Water, to cover		
Hard margarine (or butter), softened	½ cup	125 mL
Finely chopped onion	3 tbsp.	50 mL
Sherry (or fruit juice)	3 tbsp.	50 mL
Dry mustard	1 tsp.	5 mL
Salt	½ tsp.	2 mL
Ground nutmeg	¼ tsp.	1 mL
Ground cloves	⅛ tsp.	0.5 mL
Cayenne pepper	⅛ tsp.	0.5 mL
Pepper	⅛ tsp.	0.5 mL

Put chicken livers and water into medium saucepan. Bring to a boil. Cover and simmer for about 20 minutes. Drain. Grind livers in food processor or blender.

Add remaining 9 ingredients. Mix until smooth. Mound mixture on plate or spoon into oiled mold. Chill. Makes generous 2 cups (500 mL).

2 tbsp. (30 mL): 82 Calories; 6.7 g Total Fat; 167 mg Sodium; 4 g Protein; 1 g Carbohydrate; trace Dietary Fiber

SALMON PÂTÉ

An inexpensive spread with expensive smoked salmon appeal.

Cream cheese, softened	4 oz.	125 g
Grated onion	2 tsp.	10 mL
Lemon juice	1 tsp.	5 mL
Prepared horseradish	½-1 tsp.	2-5 mL
Salt	⅛ tsp.	0.5 mL
Liquid smoke	½ tsp.	2 mL
Canned salmon, drained, skin and round bones removed (red is best), flaked	7½ oz.	213 g
Drops of red food coloring (optional)		

Mash cream cheese, onion and lemon juice together in medium bowl. Add more or less horseradish if desired. Mix in salt and liquid smoke.

Add salmon and mix well. Add food coloring for appearance. Chill several hours before using. Serve with assorted crackers, toast points or toast cups. Makes about 1½ cups (375 mL).

2 tbsp. (30 mL): 63 Calories; 5.2 g Total Fat; 129 mg Sodium; 4 g Protein; trace Carbohydrate; trace Dietary Fiber

SALMON BALL: Double recipe. Shape into ball. Roll in ½ cup (125 mL) finely chopped pecans or walnuts. Top with parsley flakes. May also be rolled in a mixture of nuts and parsley.

SALMON LOG: Roll into logs a bit smaller than round crackers. Slice and place on crackers.

TUNA PÂTÉ

A well-known spread, still as good as it used to be. Garnish with parsley, chives or crushed walnuts. Serve with crackers.

Canned flaked tuna, drained	6½ oz.	184 g
Cream cheese, softened	4 oz.	125 g
Hard margarine (or butter), softened	¼ cup	60 mL
Chopped onion	½ cup	125 mL
Lemon juice	1 tsp.	5 mL
Salt	⅛ tsp.	0.5 mL
Pepper	⅛ tsp.	0.5 mL
Finely chopped nuts (optional)	½ cup	125 mL

Measure all 8 ingredients into blender. Process until smooth. Or use a beater, beating until smooth. Pack in bowl. Chill. Makes 1⅔ cups (400 mL).

2 tbsp. (30 mL): 82 Calories; 7 g Total Fat; 141 mg Sodium; 4 g Protein; 1 g Carbohydrate; trace Dietary Fiber

TUNA PINEAPPLE SPREAD

Pineapple is a wonderful addition.

Canned flaked tuna, drained	6½ oz.	184 g
Finely chopped celery	¼ cup	60 mL
Canned crushed pineapple, drained	¼ cup	60 mL
Chopped walnuts	2 tbsp.	30 mL
Salad dressing (or mayonnaise)	¼ cup	60 mL

Stir all 5 ingredients together in small bowl. Check to see if salt is needed. Makes about 1⅓ cups (325 mL).

2 tbsp. (30 mL): 60 Calories; 4 g Total Fat; 92 mg Sodium; 4 g Protein; 2 g Carbohydrate; trace Dietary Fiber

TUNA CHEDDAR SPREAD

Make the night before. A popular school or work lunch spread for sandwiches.

Canned flaked tuna, drained	6½ oz.	184 g
Grated Cheddar cheese	1 cup	250 mL
Finely chopped onion	2 tbsp.	30 mL
Sweet pickle relish	2 tbsp.	30 mL
Hard-boiled eggs, chopped	2	2
Salt	½ tsp.	2 mL
Salad dressing (or mayonnaise)	⅓ cup	75 mL

Stir all 7 ingredients together well in medium bowl. Add more salad dressing if needed for taste and for moisture. Makes about 2 cups (500 mL).

2 tbsp. (30 mL): 77 Calories; 5.7 g Total Fat; 208 mg Sodium; 5 g Protein; 1 g Carbohydrate; trace Dietary Fiber

TUNA BUTTER SPREAD

It can't get much easier than this. Smooth and tasty. Easy to increase the recipe. A little goes a long way.

Canned tuna, oil packed, drained (or add a bit of cooking oil to water-packed)	¼ cup	60 mL
Hard margarine (or butter), softened	½ cup	125 mL

Process tuna and margarine in blender for about 10 seconds. Shape into mound or pack in small bowl. Chill. Makes ⅔ cup (150 mL).

2 tbsp. (30 mL): 171 Calories; 18.2 g Total Fat; 236 mg Sodium; 2 g Protein; trace Carbohydrate; 0 g Dietary Fiber

ZIPPY TUNA SPREAD

Spread on buns and broil. Top with a cheese slice first if desired.

Canned flaked tuna, drained	6½ oz.	184 g
Salad dressing (or mayonnaise)	¼ cup	60 mL
Prepared horseradish	2 tsp.	10 mL
Lemon juice	1 tsp.	5 mL
Salt	½ tsp.	2 mL
Pepper	⅛ tsp.	0.5 mL

Mix all 6 ingredients well in small bowl. Makes about ¾ cup (175 mL).

2 tbsp. (30 mL): 84 Calories; 5.5 g Total Fat; 377 mg Sodium; 7 g Protein; 2 g Carbohydrate; trace Dietary Fiber

TUNA SPREAD

Serve with a small knife so all guests can help themselves. Tasty.

Canned white flaked tuna, water packed, drained	6$\frac{1}{2}$ oz.	184 g
Finely chopped onion	$\frac{1}{4}$ cup	60 mL
Ground walnuts	3 tbsp.	50 mL
Lemon juice	1 tsp.	5 mL
Salt	$\frac{1}{4}$ tsp.	1 mL
Pepper	$\frac{1}{4}$ tsp.	1 mL
Light salad dressing (or mayonnaise)	6 tbsp.	100 mL

Combine all 7 ingredients in medium bowl. Mix well. Chill until needed. Makes 1$\frac{1}{3}$ cups (325 mL).

2 tbsp. (30 mL): 59 Calories; 3.8 g Total Fat; 183 mg Sodium; 4 g Protein; 2 g Carbohydrate; trace Dietary Fiber

SALMON EGG SPREAD

A winning combination.

Canned salmon, drained, skin and round bones removed, flaked	7$\frac{1}{2}$ oz.	213 g
Hard-boiled eggs, chopped	2	2
Chopped celery	$\frac{1}{4}$ cup	60 mL
Parsley flakes	1 tsp.	5 mL
Lemon juice	1 tsp.	5 mL
Salt	$\frac{1}{2}$ tsp.	2 mL
Salad dressing (or mayonnaise)	$\frac{1}{3}$ cup	75 mL

Combine all 7 ingredients in medium bowl. Mix well. Makes about 1$\frac{1}{2}$ cups (375 mL).

2 tbsp. (30 mL): 75 Calories; 5.9 g Total Fat; 234 mg Sodium; 4 g Protein; 1 g Carbohydrate; trace Dietary Fiber

SALMON SPREAD

Quick and good.

Canned salmon, drained, skin and round bones removed, flaked	7$\frac{1}{2}$ oz.	213 g
Onion flakes, crushed	$\frac{1}{2}$ tsp.	2 mL
Parsley flakes	$\frac{1}{2}$ tsp.	2 mL
Salt	$\frac{1}{8}$ tsp.	0.5 mL
Salad dressing (or mayonnaise)	$\frac{1}{4}$ cup	60 mL

Mix all 5 ingredients well in medium bowl. Makes about 1 cup (250 mL).

2 tbsp. (30 mL): 79 Calories; 6.3 g Total Fat; 195 mg Sodium; 4 g Protein; 1 g Carbohydrate; trace Dietary Fiber

Cheddar cheese is one of the most common cheeses used for everyday cooking. But there is a difference between mild, medium and sharp (or old), as well as between the regular and the lower-in-fat varieties. For most recipes, medium Cheddar imparts just the right amount of zip. Because sharp (or old) Cheddar is stronger in flavor, you can use less than the recipe calls for and cut back on fat and cost.

LOBSTER SPREAD

By using this treat on open-faced buns, a little goes a long way.

Canned lobster, cartilage removed	5 oz.	142 g
Hard-boiled eggs, chopped	2	2
Chopped celery	¼ cup	60 mL
Onion flakes, crushed	1 tsp.	5 mL
Salad dressing (or mayonnaise)	1-2 tbsp.	15-30 mL

Mix all 5 ingredients in medium bowl. Makes about 1 cup (250 mL).

2 tbsp. (30 mL): 45 Calories; 2.3 g Total Fat; 92 mg Sodium; 5 g Protein; 1 g Carbohydrate; trace Dietary Fiber

SHRIMP EGG SPREAD

It is so easy to keep ingredients on hand for this sandwich filling.

Canned broken shrimp, drained	4 oz.	113 g
Hard-boiled eggs, chopped	2	2
Finely chopped celery	¼ cup	60 mL
Salad dressing (or mayonnaise)	2 tbsp.	30 mL
Lemon juice	1 tsp.	5 mL
Onion powder	¼ tsp.	1 mL
Salt	¼ tsp.	1 mL

Mash all 7 ingredients together in small bowl. Makes about 1½ cups (375 mL).

2 tbsp. (30 mL): 34 Calories; 2.1 g Total Fat; 102 mg Sodium; 3 g Protein; 1 g Carbohydrate; trace Dietary Fiber

SMOKED SALMON SPREAD

Good flavor with an economical smoked accent. Serve with crackers. May be rolled in chopped walnuts and pecans if you aren't watching calories and fat.

Low-fat cottage cheese	1 cup	250 mL
Hard margarine (or butter), softened	¼ cup	60 mL
Grated onion	1 tbsp.	15 mL
Lemon juice	1 tbsp.	15 mL
Prepared horseradish	1 tsp.	5 mL
Salt	¼ tsp.	1 mL
Liquid smoke	1 tsp.	5 mL
Canned salmon, drained, skin and round bones removed, flaked (red is best)	2 x 7½ oz.	2 x 213 g
Chopped fresh parsley	¼ cup	60 mL

Combine first 7 ingredients in small bowl. Beat together until smooth.

Add salmon and beat in slowly. Pack in shallow serving dish.

Sprinkle with parsley. Chill until ready to serve. Makes 2⅔ cups (650 mL).

2 tbsp. (30 mL): 60 Calories; 4.2 g Total Fat; 184 mg Sodium; 5 g Protein; 1 g Carbohydrate; trace Dietary Fiber

If you have tins of tuna and salmon in your cupboard, you'll never be left wondering what to serve unexpected guests. The ingredients in these spread recipes can be quickly combined to offer up as an appetizer dip with crackers for an impromptu gathering, to fill sandwiches or buns for an emergency lunch crowd, or to stuff celery sticks for a quick snack.

SHRIMP SPREAD

It is easy to keep ingredients on hand for this filling.

Canned broken shrimp, drained	4 oz.	113 g
Hard margarine (or butter)	¼ cup	60 mL
Salad dressing (or mayonnaise)	¼ cup	60 mL
Lemon juice	1½ tsp.	7 mL
Parsley flakes	1 tsp.	5 mL
Onion powder	¼ tsp.	1 mL

Mash all 6 ingredients together in small bowl. Makes generous 1 cup (250 mL).

2 tbsp. (30 mL): 103 Calories; 9.6 g Total Fat; 134 mg Sodium; 3 g Protein; 1 g Carbohydrate; trace Dietary Fiber

SHRIMP CREAM SPREAD

Cream cheese makes this extra thick and mouth watering.

Canned shrimp, drained	4 oz.	113 g
Cream cheese, softened	4 oz.	125 g
Chili sauce	1 tsp.	5 mL
Lemon juice	½ tsp.	2 mL
Worcestershire sauce	½ tsp.	2 mL
Garlic powder, pinch		
Salad dressing (or mayonnaise)	2 tbsp.	30 mL
Dill weed	⅛ tsp.	0.5 mL

Mash all 8 ingredients together in small bowl. Makes about 1 cup (250 mL).

2 tbsp. (30 mL): 85 Calories; 7.2 g Total Fat; 90 mg Sodium; 4 g Protein; 1 g Carbohydrate; trace Dietary Fiber

LAYERED CRAB SPREAD

Worth breaking any diet for.

Cream cheese, softened	8 oz.	250 g
Sour cream	½ cup	125 mL
Salad dressing (or mayonnaise)	¼ cup	60 mL
Worcestershire sauce	2 tsp.	10 mL
Onion flakes	2 tsp.	10 mL
Chili sauce	¾ cup	175 mL
Canned crabmeat, cartilage removed	2 x 4.2 oz.	2 x 120 g
Grated mozzarella cheese	2 cups	500 mL
Paprika, for garnish		
Fresh parsley, for garnish		

Mix first 5 ingredients in medium bowl. Spread evenly over 12 inch (30 cm) pizza pan.

Spread chili sauce over cheese. Layer crabmeat then cheese over top. Sprinkle with paprika. Garnish with parsley. Cover and chill. Makes 5½ cups (1.4 L).

2 tbsp. (30 mL): 56 Calories; 4.3 g Total Fat; 152 mg Sodium; 3 g Protein; 2 g Carbohydrate; trace Dietary Fiber

CRAB SPREAD

Add as much or as little dill weed as you prefer.

Canned crabmeat, drained and cartilage removed	4.2 oz.	120 g
Cream cheese, softened	4 oz.	125 g
Lemon juice	1 tsp.	5 mL
Dill weed	⅛-¼ tsp.	0.5-1 mL

Mash all 4 ingredients together in small bowl. Add dill weed to taste. Makes about 1 cup (250 mL).

2 tbsp. (30 mL): 64 Calories; 5.4 g Total Fat; 154 mg Sodium; 3 g Protein; 1 g Carbohydrate; 0 g Dietary Fiber

Measurement Tables

Throughout this book measurements are given in Conventional and Metric measure. To compensate for differences between the two measurements due to rounding, a full metric measure is not always used. The cup used is the standard 8 fluid ounce. Temperature is given in degrees Fahrenheit and Celsius. Baking pan measurements are in inches and centimetres as well as quarts and litres. An exact metric conversion is given below as well as the working equivalent (Standard Measure).

OVEN TEMPERATURES

Fahrenheit (°F)	Celsius (°C)
175°	80°
200°	95°
225°	110°
250°	120°
275°	140°
300°	150°
325°	160°
350°	175°
375°	190°
400°	205°
425°	220°
450°	230°
475°	240°
500°	260°

SPOONS

Conventional Measure	Metric Exact Conversion Millilitre (mL)	Metric Standard Measure Millilitre (mL)
1/8 teaspoon (tsp.)	0.6 mL	0.5 mL
1/4 teaspoon (tsp.)	1.2 mL	1 mL
1/2 teaspoon (tsp.)	2.4 mL	2 mL
1 teaspoon (tsp.)	4.7 mL	5 mL
2 teaspoons (tsp.)	9.4 mL	10 mL
1 tablespoon (tbsp.)	14.2 mL	15 mL

CUPS

1/4 cup (4 tbsp.)	56.8 mL	60 mL
1/3 cup (5 1/3 tbsp.)	75.6 mL	75 mL
1/2 cup (8 tbsp.)	113.7 mL	125 mL
2/3 cup (10 2/3 tbsp.)	151.2 mL	150 mL
3/4 cup (12 tbsp.)	170.5 mL	175 mL
1 cup (16 tbsp.)	227.3 mL	250 mL
4 1/2 cups	1022.9 mL	1000 mL (1 L)

PANS

Conventional Inches	Metric Centimetres
8x8 inch	20x20 cm
9x9 inch	22x22 cm
9x13 inch	22x33 cm
10x15 inch	25x38 cm
11x17 inch	28x43 cm
8x2 inch round	20x5 cm
9x2 inch round	22x5 cm
10x4 1/2 inch tube	25x11 cm
8x4x3 inch loaf	20x10x7.5 cm
9x5x3 inch loaf	22x12.5x7.5 cm

DRY MEASUREMENTS

Conventional Measure Ounces (oz.)	Metric Exact Conversion Grams (g)	Metric Standard Measure Grams (g)
1 oz.	28.3 g	28 g
2 oz.	56.7 g	57 g
3 oz.	85.0 g	85 g
4 oz.	113.4 g	125 g
5 oz.	141.7 g	140 g
6 oz.	170.1 g	170 g
7 oz.	198.4 g	200 g
8 oz.	226.8 g	250 g
16 oz.	453.6 g	500 g
32 oz.	907.2 g	1000 g (1 kg)

CASSEROLES (CANADA & BRITAIN)

Standard Size Casserole	Exact Metric Measure
1 qt. (5 cups)	1.13 L
1 1/2 qts. (7 1/2 cups)	1.69 L
2 qts. (10 cups)	2.25 L
2 1/2 qts. (12 1/2 cups)	2.81 L
3 qts. (15 cups)	3.38 L
4 qts. (20 cups)	4.5 L
5 qts. (25 cups)	5.63 L

CASSEROLES (UNITED STATES)

Standard Size Casserole	Exact Metric Measure
1 qt. (4 cups)	900 mL
1 1/2 qts. (6 cups)	1.35 L
2 qts. (8 cups)	1.8 L
2 1/2 qts. (10 cups)	2.25 L
3 qts. (12 cups)	2.7 L
4 qts. (16 cups)	3.6 L
5 qts. (20 cups)	4.5 L

Index

Mail Order Form

See reverse for list of cookbooks

QUANTITY	CODE	TITLE	PRICE EACH	PRICE TOTAL
			$	$

DON'T FORGET to indicate your FREE book(s). (see exclusive mail order offer above) PLEASE PRINT

TOTAL BOOKS (including FREE)

TOTAL BOOKS PURCHASED: $

	INTERNATIONAL		CANADA & USA	
Plus Shipping & Handling (PER DESTINATION)	$ 7.00	(one book)	$ 5.00	(1-3 books)
Additional Books (INCLUDING FREE BOOKS)	$	($2.00 each)	$	($1.00 each)
SUB-TOTAL	$		$	
Canadian residents add G.S.T(7%)			$	
TOTAL AMOUNT ENCLOSED	$		$	

The Fine Print

- Orders outside Canada must be **PAID IN US FUNDS** by cheque or money order drawn on Canadian or US bank or by credit card.
- Make cheque or money order payable to: **COMPANY'S COMING PUBLISHING LIMITED.**
- Prices are expressed in Canadian dollars for Canada, US dollars for USA & International and are subject to change without prior notice.
- Orders are shipped surface mail. For courier rates, visit our web-site: **www.companyscoming.com** or contact us: **Tel: (780) 450-6223 Fax: (780) 450-1857.**
- Sorry, no C.O.D's.

☐ MasterCard   ☐ VISA   _____
                           Expiry date

Account # _____

Name of cardholder _____

Cardholder's signature _____

Shipping Address

Send the cookbooks listed above to:

Name: _____

Street: _____

City: _____ Prov./State: _____

Country: _____ Postal Code/Zip: _____

Tel: (_____) _____

E-mail address: _____

Gift Giving

- Let us help you with your gift giving!
- We will send cookbooks directly to the recipients of your choice if you give us their names and addresses.
- Please specify the titles you wish to send to each person.
- If you would like to include your personal note or card, we will be pleased to enclose it with your gift order.
- Company's Coming Cookbooks make excellent gifts: Birthdays, bridal showers, Mother's Day, Father's Day, graduation or any occasion... collect them all!

Company's Coming cookbooks are available
at retail locations *THROUGHOUT* Canada!

See reverse for mail order

Assorted Titles	CA$19.99 Canada	US$19.99 USA & International

CODE	
EE	Easy Entertaining* (hardcover)
BE	Beef Today!

Buy any 2 cookbooks—choose a 3rd FREE of equal or less value than the lowest price paid.

Assorted Titles	CA$14.99 Canada	US$12.99 USA & International

CODE		CODE	
LFC	Low-fat Cooking*	SN	Kids-Snacks*
LFP	Low-fat Pasta*	KLU	Kids-Lunches

Buy any 2 cookbooks—choose a 3rd FREE of equal or less value than the lowest price paid.   *Available in French

Original Series	CA$12.99 Canada	US$10.99 USA & International

CODE		CODE		CODE		CODE	
SQ	150 Delicious Squares*	CO	Cookies*	PI	Pies*	BR	Breads*
CA	Casseroles*	VE	Vegetables	LR	Light Recipes*	ME	Meatless Cooking*
MU	Muffins & More*	MC	Main Courses	MI	Microwave Cooking*	CT	Cooking For Two*
SA	Salads*	PA	Pasta*	PR	Preserves*	BB	Breakfasts & Brunches*
AP	Appetizers	CK	Cakes	LCA	Light Casseroles*	SC	Slow Cooker Recipes
DE	Desserts	BA	Barbecues*	CH	Chicken, Etc.*	PZ	Pizza!*
SS	Soups & Sandwiches	DI	Dinners of the World	KC	Kids Cooking*	ODM	One-Dish Meals* ◄NEW►
HE	Holiday Entertaining*	LU	Lunches*	FS	Fish & Seafood*		Aug. '99

Buy any 2 cookbooks—choose a 3rd FREE of equal or less value than the lowest price paid.   *Available in French

Select Series	CA$9.99 Canada US$7.99 USA & International	Greatest Hits

CODE		CODE		CODE	◄NEW► Apr. '99
GB	Ground Beef*	TMM	30-Minute Meals*	BML	Biscuits, Muffins & Loaves*
B&R	Beans & Rice*	MAS	Make-Ahead Salads	DSD	Dips, Spreads & Dressings*
S&M	Sauces & Marinades*	NBD	No-Bake Desserts		

Buy any 2 cookbooks—choose a 3rd FREE of equal or less value than the lowest price paid.   *Available in French

www.companyscoming.com

COOKBOOKS

Company's Coming Publishing Limited
2311 - 96 Street
Edmonton, Alberta, Canada T6N 1G3
Tel: (780) 450-6223 Fax: (780) 450-1857
www.companyscoming.com

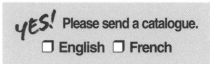